THREE THINGS YOU CAN'T ESCAPE—
DEATH, TAXES . . . AND MAINTENANCE

Jeff Campbell and The Clean Team, the San Francisco professionals who clean an entire house in 42 minutes or less, have a message you can't afford to miss: If you perform simple, routine maintenance on your household items, they will last and last—and look great too!

The problem is finding out what to do (often hopelessly complicated by poorly organized owner's manuals). How often to do it. And how to make it quick and easy. Jeff Campbell went to repair experts to find out. Now he brings you step-by-step directions for keeping everything from your air conditioner to your videotapes as good as new. You'll be astounded at what you can do to keep your hair dryer blowing and your toilets flushing.

What's the catch?

Don't put maintenance off. No arguments. No excuses. The results? No repair costs and—more important, no replacement costs—for a long, long time.

GOOD AS NEW
THE ALTERNATIVE TO OBSOLESCENCE

Books by Jeff Campbell
and The Clean Team

SPEED CLEANING
SPRING CLEANING
CLUTTER CONTROL
TALKING DIRT
GOOD AS NEW

GOOD AS NEW

Jeff Campbell
and The Clean Team

A DELL TRADE PAPERBACK

A DELL TRADE PAPERBACK

Published by
Dell Publishing
a division of
Bantam Doubleday Dell Publishing Group, Inc.
1540 Broadway
New York, New York 10036

Library of Congress Cataloging in Publication Data
Campbell, Jeff.
Good as new / Jeff Campbell and the Clean Team.
p. cm.
ISBN 0-440-50791-X
1. Home economics—Equipment and supplies—Maintenance and repair. 2. Household appliance—Maintenance and repair. 3. Household electronics—Maintenance and repair. 4. House furnishings—Maintenance and repair. I. Clean Team (San Francisco, Calif.) II. Title.
TX298.C29 1998
643'.7—dc21

97-47285
CIP

Printed in the United States of America
Published simultaneously in Canada
August 1998
10 9 8 7 6 5 4 3 2 1
FFG

Acknowledgments

If you've read any of our previous books, you may already know that Bill Redican has helped edit each of them. He has a curiosity about the world and everything and everyone in it that's astonishing and refreshing, and a memory that seemingly works as easily and as quickly for him as it does for my computer. He has been a wealth of professional information in many sections of this book, and his editing skills are once again appreciated.

I also don't know what we would have done without the maintenance knowledge provided by the craft and repair people we were lucky enough to meet and talk with. Each of them had the rare kind of knowledge that can only be attained from years of hands-on experience repairing and working with the appliances, furniture, drainpipes, faucets, CD players, air conditioners, and so forth that we all have in our homes. By sharing their knowledge, they helped solve little (and not so little) mysteries right and left that make a home seem a bit more comfortable and manageable.

Daniel Bennett is an owner of Omega Television in San Francisco. Since 1974, he has sold and serviced all types of audiovisual equipment and has seen music, sound, and images change from purely mechanical units to today's sophisticated electronics. He has a rare depth of understanding about VCRs, for example, because he sold them when they were first introduced, then started repairing those very first models when they started breaking down.

Keith Bianchi has been in the electronics business in sales, repair, and manufacturing since 1953. He had to restrain himself just so we could keep up with his stream of experienced advice. He is a wealth of knowledge and generous about sharing it. Thank you.

Lewis Downs is an independent audio expert who has been in the industry since 1963. We think he discovered and was recommending Endust as a good antistatic product for electronic audio and stereo equipment before Endust even knew it. Now that Endust has found out and introduced a specialty product just for that purpose, I only hope they send him a nice fat royalty check.

Al Hale, owner of Accurate Appliance, once again took time out of his schedule to share more of his encyclopedic knowledge about appliances. Accurate Appliance was founded by Al's dad in 1939. Al joined the business in 1953 after returning from the Korean War, and his daughter signed on and has been working with him for the last fifteen years. I think I can safely say he knows as much about appliance maintenance as anyone in the business.

Jeff Meehan is a partner of Cabrillo Plumbing in San Francisco. His company was rated number one in the country in 1996 and is consistently one of the finest plumbing and heating companies in San Francisco. That kind of great service seems rare these days and makes his achievements that much more admirable. Jeff's enthusiasm and his knowledge are much appreciated.

Tony Uruburu of McRoskey Airflex Mattress Co. works at one of the last great independent businesses in California. Thanks for sharing knowledge learned from years of experience.

After working with her on five books, I think of illustrator Axelle Fortier as an old friend. Since our books were all illustrated, I check out other illustrated books and make comparisons. No one does it better. Her illustrations help us learn and, just as important, they often make us smile. Thanks again.

Jesus Omila, Jr., in spite of his own busy schedule, once again helped us stay on schedule by keeping food on the table, drinks in the refrigerator, and the dogs patted and fed.

Also, for the fifth time, thanks to Mike Curry, Rudy Dinkel, Phil Nordeng, and my other partners and friends at The Clean Team.

Contents

1 **Death, Taxes, and Maintenance** 1

2 **Maintenance Rules** 13

3 **Alphabetical List** 19

Appendix A: Cleaning Supplies
How to Order Tools, Equipment, and Supplies 207

Appendix B: References 218

Index 223

Chapter 1

DEATH, TAXES, AND MAINTENANCE

Unfortunately, books about home maintenance are usually "how-to" or "fix-it" books. They don't appeal to me because I have little interest, or patience, in trying to fix broken things. However, I do like to take good care of things, to keep them looking like new, and to keep them running well. But once they are broken, I prefer someone else to do the fixing: someone with the proper tools, work space, temperament, experience, and time. So this is not a fix-it book. This is an avoid-having-to-fix-it-by-keeping-it-like-new book about home maintenance.

This book is a guide to taking care of the items found in most homes. We're focusing on the contents of a home and not the home itself, although it's sometimes difficult to separate the two. For example, we'll talk about how to maintain tub/shower enclosures and central air conditioners. Whether they're part of the house or part of its contents isn't clear, at least to me, but we include such items in this book if there are important maintenance issues at stake. We do not include structural items like roofs, foundations, walls, and decks, or purely personal items like jewelry and clothing.

When I started my research, I thought that much of the best information would come from owner's manuals written by manufacturers. I was dead wrong.

Sales, manufacturing, and maintenance are not comfortable bedfellows. If you ask a leather furniture salesperson, for example, "What maintenance does this leather couch need?" the answer is usually something like "What maintenance? Just wipe it with a damp cloth once in a while. Isn't the color great? How many do you want?" Salespeople know only too well that too much talk about maintenance can kill the sale. Likewise with manufacturers. Successful maintenance by consumers will extend the life of products and can ruin obsolescence projections and future replacement sales. I'm not accusing anyone of anything, but it does seem that practical maintenance doesn't get the attention it deserves.

I quickly discovered that a better resource for finding out about maintenance is from people who have spent years fixing the things other people didn't maintain properly. Plumbers know a lot about how to keep a water heater from breaking down: they fix or replace a whole lot of them. Someone who repairs major appliances knows exactly how to avoid ruining a clothes washer or dryer before its time. Much of the information in this book is from interviews with these knowledgeable people. It's the sort of information that is learned the hard way and is passed on from master to apprentice, but until now it hasn't found its way into a book for consumers.

When should you start maintenance? Even before you buy the item in question. When you make a purchase, ask pointed questions about how to care for the product you're considering. You would not believe the number of calls I get from people who have just arrived home with something new and want to know how to clean or maintain it. *Ask* the salesperson. Persist until you get a full answer—not "Cleanup is a breeze" or "This unit practically takes care of itself." You *must* know what maintenance to perform and how to clean it (and with what product), as well as how often to schedule maintenance and cleaning operations. Besides that, ask if it will fade, stain, dent, scratch, rust, crack, splinter, shrink, peel, or rot.

Also, before you make a purchase, consider how much time this item will be adding to the total time spent maintaining the household. Each decision adds a bit more to the total unless you also get rid of something. Unless you manage these maintenance demands, ultimately the amount of time required will be more than is available. Certain building materials, design elements, and new possessions require much more maintenance time than others. For example, shiny surfaces magnify every little fingerprint, whereas fingerprints on brushed surfaces are not even noticeable. Here's a partial list of high-maintenance items:

- Glass doors
- Glass furniture
- Clear glass shower doors
- Any shower enclosure
- Fiberglass showers with sand-grain floors
- Unfinished wood
- Soft wood
- Carpets in bathrooms and kitchens
- Dried flower arrangements
- Silk flower arrangements
- Tiny hexagonal floor tiles (in many old San Francisco homes, unfortunately)

- Black and white floors
- White grout—especially on counters and floors
- Gold or brass plumbing fixtures
- Brass anything else—whether lacquered or not
- Collections of anything small displayed in the open
- Collections of anything large displayed in the open
- Chandeliers
- Clear glass light fixtures
- Windows that can't be opened to clean
- Miniblinds
- Highly textured floors, walls, ceilings, or wallpaper
- Glossy, shiny floors
- Carpets that show vacuum marks
- Light- or dark-colored carpets
- Floor-to-ceiling mirrors
- Large bathroom mirrors
- Bare aluminum window frames
- Practically any fabric-covered furniture

- Fabric lampshades
- Wicker furniture
- Piles of pillows on furniture
- Cheap: Plastic that scratches
  Carpet that doesn't hold up
  Paint that can't be washed repeatedly
- Grouted tile counters
- Intricate: Beds
  Cabinets
  Knobs
  Lampshades

Obviously you can't, nor would most of us want to, avoid everything on this list. But pick items for your home critically and judiciously. Otherwise you'll spend excessive time on maintenance efforts for years to come.

One way to measure the difference between high-quality products and poor-quality products is the additional time it takes to maintain the latter. Buy as good a quality as you can afford in order to reduce maintenance time. Delay the purchase, if you must, to get items that will last. You'll remember and appreciate the quality of your purchase long after you've forgotten its price.

Once home, well-maintained possessions retain greater value, are more reliable (they don't leak, don't skip, aren't too hot or too cold, too fast or too slow), look better, and continue to be more enjoyable as the years pass by. To give yourself an idea of how valuable maintenance can be, take a stroll through your home and add up the cost of the things you see—stove, refrigerator, CDs, washer, carpets, furniture, books, art, and so forth. Proper maintenance means that should you decide to sell everything and move to Grenada, you'll get full value. Without it, you may have to pay someone to haul your possessions away.

Well-maintained things also reduce the number of crises you'll have to face. An air conditioner serviced at the start of the warm season is less likely to break down on the hottest weekend of the summer when the house is full of sweltering guests. Postponing maintenance means that a small problem will inevitably blossom into a more expensive, inconvenient, full-blown nuisance someday.

Many of us are bothered by the feeling that we ought to be doing something to maintain our leather couch, CD player, water heater, or air conditioner. However, we aren't sure if this is just meaningless guilt or a genuine call to action. If it is indeed the latter, we usually don't know exactly what the activity is or when it's called for. This book will help on both counts.

This book will not, however, make you an expert on air conditioners, water heaters, CD players, or any of the other entries in Chapter 3. Rather, it will teach you what maintenance is needed to keep such things running well and/or looking good for the longest time possible. The philosophy is similar to the one I use when talking with computer experts about new software for my office computers. I tell them, "I don't want to know how it works. I just want to know which button to push." Inevitably, I have to remind them of this once or twice as the conversation proceeds. In this book, I have tried to follow my own advice and relate only what is needed to maintain an item. And that's where I stop. If you want to become an armchair expert on air conditioners, for example, you can find books about almost every aspect of them. What's previously been difficult to find is a book *only* about maintaining such things in the home.

Some of the maintenance information included in this book can be found in various owner's manuals. But let's face it: almost no one reads such manuals. They're usually overwhelming, poorly written, shoddily organized, and lacking concrete advice. For example, the first two and one-half pages of my "Residential Instruction Manual for Gas Water Heaters" consist of nothing but warnings. Then the manual moves on to describe a "typical installation" with a uselessly general illustration accompanied by three more warnings. Then comes "Locating the New Water Heater" (a short paragraph), followed by a caution and five more warnings in bold letters and boxes. It's not clear to me what the distinction between a "caution" and a "warning" is, and I'm not sure I would care if I found out.

However, this is litigious America, and much corporate activity is devoted to avoiding and defending against product liability lawsuits. Warnings and cautions seem to be the first line of defense. This is all well and good, but I've yet to meet anyone who has read them. And all the warnings seem to have elbowed out the down-to-earth practical advice that we're all looking for.

By the way, since it might occur to someone to sue me as well, I have come up with my own warning:

> ***Hey!* The maintenance instructions in this book are generic and do not include important warnings and specific instructions contained in the owner's manual for the specific product at hand. You may be exposed to dangerous risks without those warnings and instructions. Before you proceed, please review the owner's manual or contact the manufacturer or other professional to protect yourself against injury or death if you have any doubt, question, or hesitation about any procedure contained in this book.**

After warnings, the next line of defense seems to be to tell consumers to perform certain maintenance chores so often that it seems obvious the advice is meant to shift blame from the manufacturer to the consumer if a problem ever arises. For example, manufacturers of fire extinguishers tell us to check the pressure gauge once a month. Do they tell us that because they stay up nights worrying about us, or because in the event of a fire they can claim it was the fault of the consumer who, like most all of us, hadn't checked the pressure on the fire extinguisher for a year? They sort of have us over a barrel. We don't want to risk our family's safety, but we have only so much time in the day. Is it really, truly, absolutely necessary that we all mark our calendars every month for the rest of our lives to check the pressure on every fire extinguisher we own? Or are manufacturers giving us busywork while trying to ensure that they are protected from phantom lawsuits? Add in checkups on water heaters, refrigerators, freezers, electrical devices of all kinds, and pretty soon there would be no time left in the day at all. In this book, we'll offer suggestions on how to live with generalized instructions and how to personalize them to your home and to your life-style—a refreshing dollop, we trust, of common sense. Most of us want to take care of our things, but we don't have any time to waste unnecessarily.

When you buy a house, especially if it's a used one, get as much information as you can from the builders or sellers about things in the house like the furnace, air conditioner, refrigerator, stove, washer, and dryer. What maintenance has been performed to date? Ask for any owner's manuals. Ask what products have been used on wood floors and if tile and grout in the house have been sealed. Ask for the names and phone numbers of tradespeople such as plumbers, electricians, and appliance-repair people who are familiar with the appliances in the house. While you're at it, ask for the names and phone numbers of roofers, gardeners, and any others that you may want to consult in the future.

Despite the poor quality and the lack of helpful information in many owner's manuals, save them all. Also save warranties, sales slips, and other literature that comes with the things you buy. Read them or not, but create a hanging file for them in your file cabinet (*Clutter Control,* see Appendix B). You never know! Every once in a while manufacturers slide some valuable information into those papers. Besides, when your sister's children accidentally reprogram your VCR, you will have to read how to undo whatever they did to make the sound disappear.

The two main chapters go from the general to the specific. Chapter 2 reviews maintenance rules that apply to most household situations. Chapter 3 provides an alphabetical list of items likely to be found in your home. So if you would like to know what maintenance should be performed on your refrigerator, look under "R." For better or worse, that's where our responsibility ends. The next step is up to you, but it will be much easier to take that step with the confidence that knowledge provides.

NOTE: As in our previous books on cleaning (*Speed Cleaning, Spring Cleaning, Clutter Control,* and *Talking Dirt*), when we mention a cleaning product, we will use the name of the product The Clean Team uses when cleaning homes in San Francisco. (Established in 1979, The Clean Team has long been San Francisco's busiest housecleaning service, cleaning homes nearly twenty thousand times a year.) So, for example, if a maintenance step calls for a heavy-duty liquid cleaner, we'll say "Red Juice." Now, this may be a bit annoying if you don't have any Red Juice or wouldn't know Red Juice from a cheap Chianti. To avoid this problem, in Appendix A we further explain any cleaning supplies or products we mention. We compare Red Juice to other products in the same category. In this case, Red Juice is a heavy-duty liquid cleaner of the same general type as Simple Green, Formula 409, Fantastik, and so forth. The Clean Team tried those products (and many others), and Red Juice was the one we thought performed best in this category. Don't get us wrong. You don't have to have Red Juice to do anything you read about in this book. You can substitute any number of other commonly available cleaning products. Just check in Appendix A if we mention a cleaner you're not familiar with, and you'll find the names of similar products you probably already have right now.

If you would like to know more about any of the products The Clean Team has found to be best, please ask for a free catalog by calling 1-800-238-2996. We'll pop one in the mail to you the same day. And please call the same number if you have a cleaning question. We'll do our best to provide you with a professional answer for your dilemma.

Chapter 2

MAINTENANCE RULES

As in our other books, we've distilled a few core principles or operating rules that have emerged as we've done our research on this subject. We hope they will be helpful in situations not mentioned in this book so you'll be more equipped to develop maintenance solutions tailored to your specific household.

Rule 1: ***Schedule your maintenance.*** Most actual (as opposed to imaginary) maintenance is scheduled for a definite date, not "next month," "when I get around to it," or "as soon as I have a free Saturday." Indefinite dates never actually arrive, and, as everyone knows, there is no such thing as a free Saturday. Some maintenance dates are determined by the season—for example, servicing the air conditioner before the warm season starts. But some dates are determined by your home and living style. If the manufacturer tells everyone in the world to clean the freezer's condenser coils every three months, test that advice for yourself. Go ahead and dust the coils (see **Freezers,** Chapter 3) and then *check* them in three months. If the coils are dirty again, clean them again. But if not, recheck monthly until they really are dirty. Now you have a maintenance interval that's more meaningful than what the manufacturer said. Enter it into a maintenance journal (see Rule 13).

Rule 2: ***Treating your belongings with care will reduce maintenance.*** In many cases, patterns of daily use are more important than maintenance in determining how long something will last. Be gentle. You can break almost anything if you try—purposely or not. Little plastic pieces are sometimes the most important part of something and are easily broken off. An example is my hummingbird feeder. If that plastic piece is broken, the whole feeder is useless. I know you're *always* in a hurry, but habitually stuffing twenty-six pounds of laundry into an eighteen-pound-capacity washer instead of doing two smaller loads will take years off the life of the washer.

Rule 3: ***All things are not created equal as far as maintenance goes.*** By this I mean that things used heavily need more attention than things used lightly. If you maintain the entire carpet on the same schedule, traffic areas will be worn out before the balance of the carpet shows any wear at all. Also, over time, low-quality items often cost more to maintain, wear out more quickly, must be refinished, repaired, or cleaned more often, and must be replaced more quickly than quality items—which means they also end up costing more anyway. Don't settle for high-maintenance, low-cost items if waiting will allow you to afford better quality.

Rule 4: ***Don't buy any product without knowing exactly what care it needs, how often it needs it, what cleaning it needs, and what product(s) to use.***

Rule 5: ***Cleaning is a major part of preventive maintenance and is often the cure for failures or problems.*** For example, the most common problem with CD players is skipping. The cause is almost invariably a dirty disc or laser lens. The cure is cleaning in either case.

Rule 6: ***Water is the enemy.*** Even seemingly small amounts of water are more dangerous than dirt to your house. A little drip behind the washer or a tiny leak in a shower will eventually ruin the drywall, then the studs, flooring, and joists. Ditto for water oozing in around windows, doors, and other openings to the outside. A leak is almost guaranteed to cost thousands of dollars of damage if ignored. Some of that water will eventually make its way to the frame underneath and start the inevitable process of deterioration. And water that soaks the soil underneath will attract termites and all sorts of other nefarious creatures.

Rule 7: ***Ditto for direct sunlight.*** Keep most things out of direct sunlight. Carpets, wood floors, and many fibers fade; leather dries out; fibers are weakened; plastic warps; paper yellows.

Rule 8: ***The more moving parts, the more imperative it is to keep the item clean.*** If a unit has moving parts, dirt is particularly dangerous. Moving parts also need lubrication unless factory-sealed.

Rule 9: ***If you find yourself even thinking about it, it's time to change filters.*** It is just about impossible to change filters too often. They usually aren't expensive, so *replace* rather than clean regularly.

Rule 10: ***Buy good floor mats.*** You've probably heard it before, but everything they say about "good" floor mats is true. They can prevent lots of dirt from making it to places where it can cause damage. Good floor mats are *not* the cute little ones made of hemp or rubber that say WELCOME. Good mats are the ones you see both outside and inside the doors of banks and other public buildings. They are big enough to take several steps on. They are made from nylon fiber or polypropylene fiber with heavy rubber backing, and they can be easily vacuumed to remove accumulated dirt. They belong both outside *and* inside all entrances to the home. Sources include janitorial supply houses and The Clean Team Catalog (1-800-328-2996).

Rule 11: ***Take advantage of a move or repair.*** Anytime you disassemble something or move something heavy out of place, clean everything carefully before reassembling or moving it back into position. So when the refrigerator is pulled out to be repaired, clean the floor where the refrigerator was and vacuum the coils, the motor, and anything else that can't ordinarily be reached.

Rule 12: ***When it doubt, seal it.*** If instructions say to apply a protective seal on a product, do so. Grout of all sorts will last longer, stay cleaner, and resist stains and water damage far better if you do. So will various types of tile and natural stone products. Like making a bed or painting a room, sealants must be renewed at regular intervals.

Rule 13: ***Keep notes or a journal of your maintenance activities.*** When you learn how often different maintenance chores need to be done in your home, write it down. Date each entry so you know for sure when it's time to do it again. Include notes on anything that looks odd or suggests the possibility of a future problem. Identify major problems so that needed repairs can be scheduled in advance. You can use a simple three-ring binder or spiral-bound notebook and file it with your monthly bills so you have it in your hot little hands regularly to check for upcoming maintenance activities.

Chapter 3

ALPHABETICAL LIST

Air, Indoor

Today's homes are sealed much tighter than older ones, which slows the rate of air exchange with the great outdoors. This is fine if the great outdoors happens to be 20° below zero. But without fresh air, a buildup of materials from furniture, carpets, construction, pets, and/or smoke can cause what would certainly be called smog were it outdoors. Improve the quality of the air in your home by:

- regularly changing the filter(s) in the heating, ventilating, and air-conditioning systems;
- opening windows and doors whenever practicable; and
- using exhaust fans routinely if your kitchen and/or bathrooms are so equipped. Clean or replace the filters in these exhaust fans on a preventive schedule.

Another potentially dangerous buildup in household air is moisture. Too much moisture promotes mold and mildew growth on and in clothes, walls, closets, and basements. Some research indicates that mold, when it can't escape from today's tight-as-a-submarine buildings, is the source of interior pollutants with the most widespread impact on health. Cooking, laundering, and showering can add two gallons or more of water a day to a house (Michigan State University Extension). Cool air holds less moisture than warm air, so you can rid air of moisture by: (1) turning on the air conditioner, or (2) heating the house for a short time and then quickly opening doors and windows to exchange the moisture-laden air for cooler and drier air. Granules that absorb moisture are sold in hardware stores and are good for damp closets, but they have limited impact on an area the size of a room.

Dehumidifiers reduce moisture in the air in much the same way that an air conditioner does.

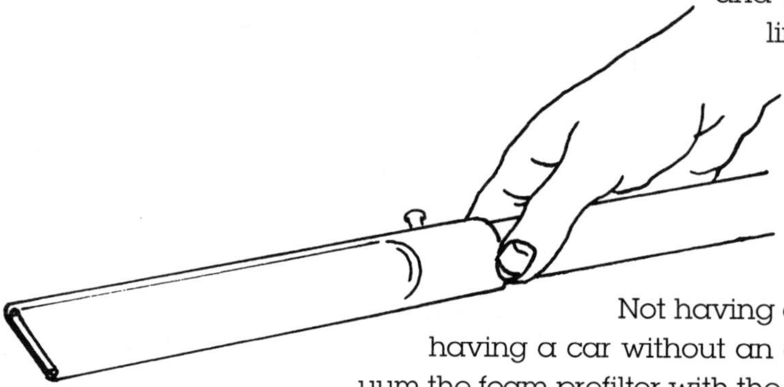

Air Cleaners

Not having a *clean* filter in an air *cleaner* is kind of like having a car without an engine—it misses the whole point. So vacuum the foam prefilter with the crevice tool at least once a month; or wash it with dish soap and water, rinse, and let dry. At the same time, vacuum or wipe inside the cabinet with a dampened cloth.

Most manufacturers suggest: (1) cleaning ion-emitting needles every other month or so with a cotton swab dipped in alcohol; (2) replacing activated charcoal filters every three to six months; and (3) replacing HEPA filters once a year.

Run air cleaners continuously to get the greatest benefit. Position them near the source of dust if you can. The cleaned air will blow toward the middle or most-used part of the room.

Audiotapes See **Cassette Tapes.**

Bathtubs

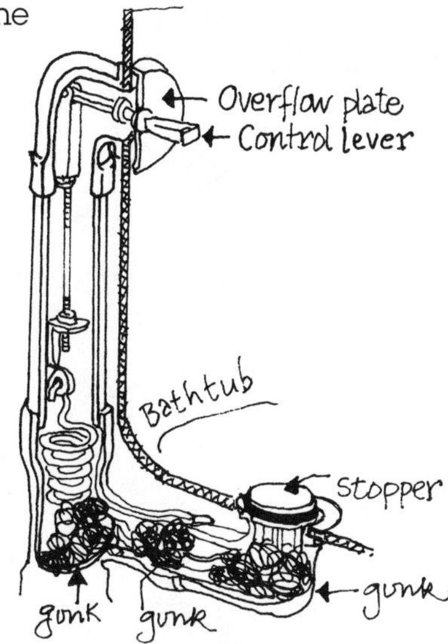

Most tub drains become clogged sooner or later with hair, even though most tubs have a removable plug in the drain. Clean the hair from the plug once or twice a year (depending on how quickly it starts to clog) by twisting or pulling the drain plug out, or by removing the lever that operates the drain plug's closing mechanism. Now you can pull out the stem and clean the hair (which has now turned into gunk) from the end of it.

Protect the tub from damage from tools, paint, trash, and so on,

when redecorating or remodeling by laying down a few towels or a tarp. Don't walk in the tub with shoes to hang shower curtains. Any grit—and there always seems to be some—caught between the tub and a shoe can cause a scratch in a moment.

Tub/Shower Enclosures, Caulking. Water or moisture in the wrong places is a threat to your house (see Rule 6). A common place for water to creep into areas of the house where it doesn't belong is around the tub or shower. Inspect the caulk every so often when you shower. Check the joints for cracks or separation between the tub and shower, between the tub/shower and the wall, and around the drain.

Caulk is one of the main defenses against moisture, but it was never intended to last as long as structural materials like wood and metal. However, if caulk is applied *under* building materials as the house is being built (so it isn't exposed to the air), it can last thirty to fifty years. Replace the caulk in any tub or shower joints when you notice it peeling, discoloring, shrinking, or developing gaps.

It is not particularly difficult to recaulk. The most difficult step is arranging to remove the bathroom from service for a few days. Contemplation can be converted to action by reminding yourself of the damage water does to your walls and floors *and* that your homeowner's policy will not pay for the repairs.

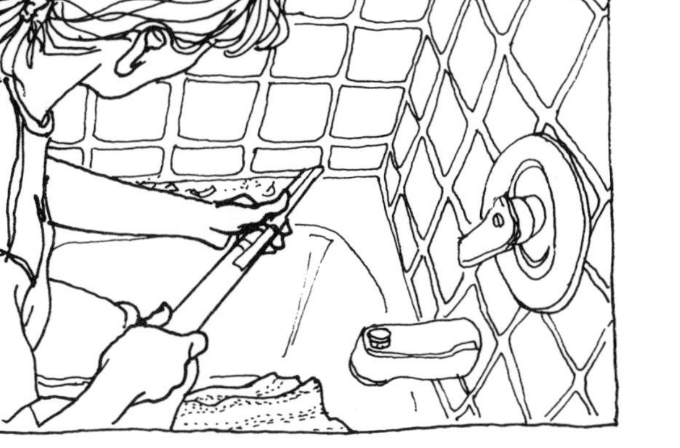

Before you start, clean the tub/shower enclosure thoroughly. Get rid of any soap scum buildup or hard-water spots, especially where you will be working. Then protect the tub with towels, a blanket, or a drop cloth. Remove all the old caulk you can, using a putty knife, screwdriver, metal pick, or a pair of pliers to pull it loose. Use a screwdriver or metal pick to rough up the surface of any caulk you can't remove so the new caulk will adhere better. Try not to stab yourself or scratch the surrounding surfaces as you do.

Then vacuum with the crevice tool to remove loose caulk, dust, and debris. Wipe the area to be recaulked with a solvent (like alcohol) to remove oils and other films. If mildew was growing anywhere in or around the old caulk, spray the area thoroughly with bleach. (Use undiluted household chlorine bleach or dilute it with up to ten parts water.) Rinse thoroughly after a few minutes with plain water, keeping excess water out

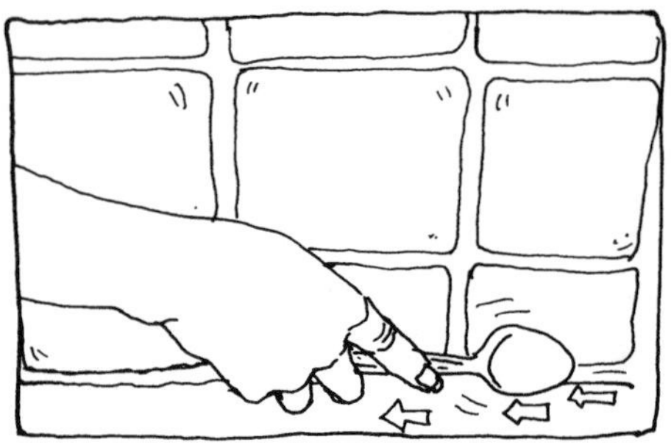

of the newly exposed cracks. It will take a very long time to dry if excessive rinse water runs into the spaces that caulk used to fill. So take a break while it dries completely—usually overnight. If you're in a hurry, use a hair dryer to shorten the drying time, but don't recaulk before all surfaces to be treated are absolutely dry.

Caulks are now available that are pressurized and dispense without a caulking gun. Besides your not having to purchase or fuss with a caulking gun, they also make it a bit easier to get professional-looking results. For tub/shower enclosures, the best type of caulk is silicone because of its high flexibility and low shrinkage. If mildew grows in the shower even occasionally, choose a caulk with a mildewcide that will help subdue the mildew population for a year or so. There are dozens of different kinds of caulks to choose from. Shop where you trust the salespeople, explain exactly what you're going to do, and then buy the most expensive caulk if there are several to choose from. (It's worth it.)

Begin caulking at one end of the least visible joint. (Don't caulk the most visible area until you get the hang of it.) A continuous bead of caulk gives the best-looking results. Usually what stops you from applying a bead continuously is something in your way. So move stuff out of the way and do a dry run from one end of the tub to the other. Then fill the joint evenly without overfilling. If you must stop in the middle, overlap slightly and start again.

Produce a smooth finish by running your wet finger or a plastic spoon over the fresh bead of caulk. Depending on the type of caulk and temperature, caulk skins over quite quickly, so try not to dillydally. Rewet your finger as needed to avoid pulling the caulk out of position.

Allow the caulk to cure according to label directions (usually thirty-six hours) before using the tub/shower. **Note:** Curing should not be sped up with heat.

Batteries

Alkaline. Alkaline batteries can leak acid even if they're unused. One appliance manufacturer reports that they've seen batteries fail and leak two years *before* the expiration date! If you have batteries in equipment such as a camcorder, take them out if you don't plan to use the equipment within a week or so. Likewise, if you're using the AC adapter instead of the batteries, take the batteries out or check on them weekly. The damage that acid can cause to electronic circuitry far outweighs the inconvenience of removing or checking on the batteries.

Ni-Cad (rechargeable). According to Panasonic, today's nickel-cadmium batteries are virtually immune to "battery memory" problems caused by using a battery for a short time and then recharging it. They report that studies now show that repeated charging following a partial discharge can actually increase the battery capacity by as much as 10 percent. Don't use them immediately after charging while they're still hot, and store them in a cool place when not in use. An unused corner of your refrigerator or wine cellar would be dandy.

If you haven't used your Ni-Cad batteries for six months or more, you may have to discharge and recharge them several times before the batteries are fully restored.

NOTE: The battery contacts of almost any battery-powered gadget don't have to be very dirty to interrupt the trickle of current. They can be cleaned with an ordinary pencil eraser, silver polish on a polishing cloth, emery board, or very fine sandpaper. (Rub gently!) Clean both ends of the battery as well as the battery contacts inside the appliance. If the batteries are failing to recharge for no apparent reason, or if replacement batteries don't seem to work, this is the first thing to try—*before* taking an appliance in for repair or tearing it apart. It may save you a trip or a few gray hairs. Manage pencil erasure droppings so they aren't left in the unit. They could interfere with things that have delicate moving parts (e.g., tape recorders, CD players, etc.).

Bedding

Blankets. To reduce the number of times you have to launder blankets and quilts, vacuum them with the brush or furniture attachment a few times a year. Store unused quilts in large pillowcases, but not in plastic bags that don't allow air to circulate.

As long as the blankets are labeled as washable, pretreat spots and stains with a laundry prewash agent or with Red Juice. Keeping in mind the exception that you should wash only one blanket at a time, follow the instructions for washing pillows (see **Pillows,** page 29). Soak a very dirty blanket for fifteen minutes or more before starting the wash cycle, and squeeze it by hand a few times as it soaks.

The procedure for drying blankets depends more on their type of fabric. Here's what Michigan State University Extension sources recommend for drying wool blankets:

Dry . . . on the high temperature setting. To absorb moisture and dry a blanket more quickly, place 3 or 4 dry towels in dryer. Preheat towels for 3 to 5 minutes. This helps absorb moisture, dry blankets rapidly and avoid pilling caused by long tumbling. Place the blanket in the dryer with the warm towels. Set dryer control for about 20 minutes. Check the blanket after 10 minutes. Remove while still slightly damp to avoid shrinkage. Place blanket on flat surface or over two [clothes] lines. . . . Stretch it to its original shape. When the blanket is completely dry, brush gently (with a soft brush) to raise nap. Press binding with a cool iron, if needed.

Hang the blanket over the shower door if you—like me—don't have those two clotheslines to drape it over.

For cotton and synthetic blankets, set the dryer to permanent press, and remove the blanket from the dryer as soon as it stops. Restretch to its original size, if necessary, before it cools off completely.

Blankets, Electric. Laundering is easy to do, so don't put it off until the blanket won't come clean. Follow the manufacturer's laundering instructions. If you don't have them anymore, start by presoaking the blanket in the washing machine for fifteen minutes in laundry detergent and warm water. (One of the warnings in my owner's manual was to tell me to unplug it before washing it. What was I going to do? Add an extension cord so it would reach to the washing machine?)

Use your hands to squeeze soap and water through the blanket. Then launder on the gentle cycle for one to five minutes. It can be put through the spin cycle, but set the cycle to gentle as well. Dry it on the lowest temperature setting for ten minutes and check. Remove it while still damp, and let it air-dry over the shower door or two parallel clotheslines. Have someone help you gently pull it back into shape while it is still damp and again when it's laid on the bed.

NOTE: Most electric blankets will shrink considerably if you dry them too long. Too much heat can cause electrical problems as well.

Down Comforters. Down comforters can be washed the same way as pillows (see below). The only problem is that many home washing machines aren't big enough to accommodate one. Take the comforter to a Laundromat and use an oversize washer.

Pillows. Birds preen their feathers every day, and it's probably smart for humans to take the hint. So give your feather pillows a good "fluff" every time you make the bed. Wash the pillowcase and, if there is one, the removable cover regularly to prevent dirt and body oils from migrating to the ticking or filling. Leaving pillows in a crushed position can permanently damage the loft of a down feather, so don't wad them up or store them under heavy linens for long.

It's not unusual for feather pillows to be discarded without ever being washed, when, in fact, washing every couple of years is a good idea. As long as the label says "washable," they can go directly into the washing machine. Select regular agitation and spin cycles and use warm water and detergent. If you have a top-loading machine, first fill the machine, add the detergent, and either agitate manually or let the machine agitate briefly to mix the detergent and water. Then add the pillows. Push them down into the water because they will float. If you have a front-loading machine, add the soap, then the pillows, and then fill with water. Wash two or three of them in the same load. Let them soak for ten minutes or so and swish them around a couple of times during this period. Now let the machine agitate for five minutes or so before moving the dial ahead to the first spin cycle or to the rinse cycle if there's only one spin cycle. (Important!) *First* push in the dial, or otherwise turn off the machine, then turn the dial ahead to the new setting before pulling it back out again to restart the cycle. Let it go through the rinse and remaining spin cycles. Set it for an extra rinse if available. (If not, and if the pillow still seems soapy to you, rinse again in the washer or sink and then put it through a final spin cycle.)

Pillows take a long time to dry, so be patient and start early. Set the dryer to low. Stop the dryer every half hour or so and give the pillows a good shake to help dry, reshape, and refluff them. Be patient and try not to imagine they are dry before they really are. They must be completely dry or they will be vulnerable to mildew.

Blenders

Blenders are designed for speed, not power (like a food processor), so they are easily overloaded. In other words, they can't move around a heavy volume of food. Be gentle.

To keep the bank of buttons from sticking, clean them by spraying very lightly—misting, really—with Red Juice. Use a toothbrush to agitate the surfaces of the buttons, the sides of the buttons, and the area between the buttons. Dry with a cleaning cloth. Drape the cleaning cloth over the toothbrush to dry hard-to-reach areas like the ones between the buttons.

Disassemble the blender jar to clean. When disassembling or reassembling, protect the rubber gasket from damage. Nicks make the blender leak. Replace the gasket if it's dried out, cracked, or otherwise suspect.

Books and Bookshelves

Books should be removed from bookshelves and their tops vacuumed once a year or so (more often if the room is very dusty and less often if not). Do this in a methodical way. Start at one end of the highest bookshelf. Grab a handful of books with one hand and tilt them outward so their tops can be vacuumed with the brush attachment held in the other hand. Keep the books closed so dust won't fall into them, and vacuum from the spine to the edge of the book. Because of the design of some shelves, you first may have to slide the books partially off the shelf before you can tilt them forward. If the books are too tightly packed to allow this, remove a few books to make some room. Set these books on the next shelf or on the floor until you're done with the shelf.

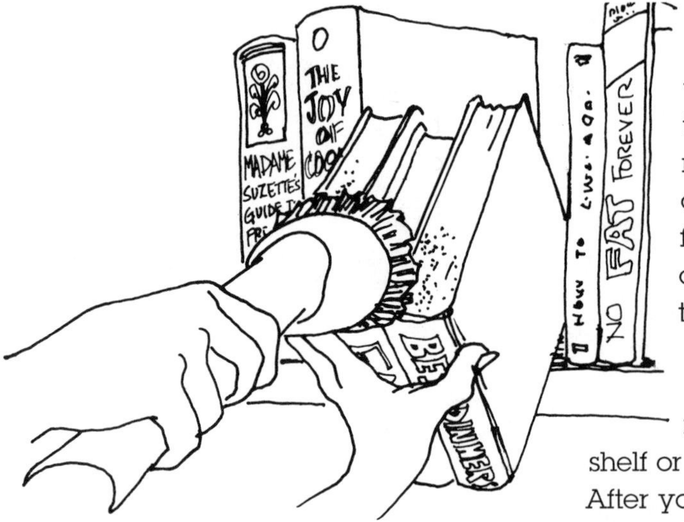

After you've vacuumed the tops of the books in a shelf, push them as deep into the shelf as they will go to expose the front part of the shelf, and wipe that exposed area with a Red Juice–dampened cleaning cloth. Finally, pull the books back out into their proper position and move on to the next shelf. (An option is to remove the books completely, vacuum them, wipe the shelves, and restack the books. But since the books prevent dust from reaching most of the shelf area, this isn't usually necessary except on shelves with collectibles instead of books or in the case of unusually fragile books.)

Another enemy of books is moisture. So maintenance includes monitoring for possible mildew growth—especially if you have warm, damp summers. Check books occasionally for mildew growth on pages and covers—leather covers in particular. If mildew is a problem, install a light bulb or chemical dehumidifying crystals in any enclosed bookshelves and/or consider installing a room or central dehumidifier or air conditioner. (And check the roof, walls, or foundation for sources of leaks or condensation.)

To treat established mildew spots, a dab of hydrogen peroxide or alcohol may help. Use in moderation (a cotton swab is a good idea) and blot up any excess quickly. If the mildew has spread deep into the pages, sprinkle diatomaceous earth (available at a garden-supply store or plant nursery) in the page, leave the book closed for several days, and then shake and vacuum the book out. Serious mildew infestation is a job for a book/paper restorer (*Cleaning and Caring for Books,* see Appendix B).

Butcher Block Surfaces

A good one—preferably made of a hardwood like birch—will last long enough to be able to hand down to the grandkids (if they ever develop an interest in cooking). The secret is maintenance, of course. Don't apply a hard finish like polyurethane or varnish. Use an oil finish instead. There are differing opinions on which oil to use. Some prefer mineral oil because other oils (boiled linseed, vegetable, etc.) can turn rancid. I have always had great luck, however, with walnut oil. I like the feel of it, it gives the wood a beautiful finish, it lasts a long time, and it has never turned rancid in my fifteen or so years of experience with it. Besides, walnut oil came from a hardwood tree to begin with. I keep a bottle of it handy for the butcher block, which means it's also available when a recipe calls for it.

To season a new butcher block, apply walnut oil with a paper towel. Be liberal with the oil, and cover the top and four sides while the block is resting on paper towels over a few layers of newspaper on the counter. It doesn't matter whether you apply it with the grain or across the grain. Wait an hour or more, and repeat. Keep applying until the wood seems equally saturated (usually several times). Then wipe thoroughly with a cleaning cloth or more paper towels, turn the block over, and repeat on the bottom.

Here's how to get a well-used butcher block ready for a coat of walnut oil. Scrub the surface with dish soap, hot water, and a white pad or a soap-impregnated steel wool pad. Rinse and let dry. If the surface is rough, sand lightly, but unless this is a restoration, don't try to make the surface like new again. Wash once again after sanding and let dry. If the surface is still heavily stained or too dark for your liking, apply a solution of 50 percent bleach and water to the surface. (You can use up to full-strength bleach if you prefer.) Use gloves and avoid the fumes. Use the same plastic scrub pad to work the bleach into the wood. Wait a few minutes, then rinse, wash one more time with soap and water, rinse again, and let dry. Repeat this step to further lighten the wood. Do a final touch-up with fine sandpaper, if needed, and now you're ready to apply walnut oil as just described. Whew.

Wash the block after each use with dish soap and water, rinse, and wipe dry. Some of the walnut oil is removed each time the block is cleaned, so reapply additional walnut oil as needed—usually every few months or so—whenever it passes the particular threshold of drabness or dryness that bothers you.

Cabinets

During normal housecleaning, cabinets are just wiped around the handles, where fingerprints are most likely to appear. The rest of the cabinet surface—especially in the case of kitchen cabinets—needs a deep cleaning once a year or so. The specific cleaning steps vary depending on whether the cabinets have a natural wood finish, are painted, or are metal. If the cabinets aren't cleaned when needed, especially in the kitchen where grease is interacting with the finish of the cabinets, they may have to be refinished or repainted. In addition to this yearly cleaning, maintenance includes checking that hinge screws are snug and lightly lubricating the hinges with Teflon spray or WD-40.

If a screw has stripped the wood and can't be tightened any longer, here's what to do. After removing the screw, stuff the hole with wooden matches or toothpicks, and break them off flush with the surface. Now insert the screw and tighten. If the holes are so short that the matches or toothpicks won't stay in the hole, glue them in place before you insert the screw. Alternatively, you can use longer screws or fill the holes completely with epoxy putty and start over again.

Protectors for cabinet doors are designed to cushion their stop against the door frame of the cabinet. These protectors often fall off or otherwise mysteriously disappear over time. Without them, the cabinets are noisier and the screws and hinges more likely to loosen or fail. Check how many are missing when you do a heavy cleaning of the cabinets, and then get replacements at a hardware store. They are available as self-adhesive plastic, rubber, felt, or cork dots. Take a sample so you can pick one that has the same material and thickness as the existing protectors.

Camcorders See **Video Camcorders.**

Cameras

Many maintenance problems with cameras are really accidents that happen as we're prowling about trying to get interesting photos. Use your camera case and its carrying strap to minimize the risks. Dirt and moisture cause many other maintenance problems. Go to extravagant lengths to keep them both out of the camera and off the film.

We all know we're supposed to remove the batteries when storing a camera. But most of us ignore this eminently sensible advice, so when you change batteries, at least clean the contact points with an eraser or similar means (see **Batteries**).

Everyone also knows they're supposed to clean their camera. There's no easy way out of this one, but fortunately it doesn't take long. First, and this is important, remove hard grit with a few blasts of canned air (available at camera or electronics stores), a lungful of air, or the lens-cleaning blower brush lying unused in the junk drawer. Then, using a soft cloth, clean the lens, the viewfinder, and the face of the electric eye. Purists gasp, but I treat it just like a pair of glasses. First I breathe on the part to be cleaned and then I wipe it with the cloth. There are special lens-cleaning fluids and lens tissues available where cameras are sold. Take a couple of minutes to perform this chore occasionally but regularly. If your camera accepts filters, install a haze filter over the lens to protect it.

When you get word that your first grandchild is going to perform at the White House and you haven't used your camera for some time, take it out and test it. Clean the battery contacts and replace the batteries, or at the very least purchase a spare set—not a bad idea in any event. Give yourself time to get it fixed if anything is amiss.

Can Openers

The cutting wheel should be cleaned every few months. Usually it will pull away from the body of an electric opener and can then be put in the dishwasher. If further cleaning is necessary, use a toothbrush and Red Juice or fine steel wool. The cutting wheel will probably last a bit longer if you lubricate it with some cooking oil after cleaning. Dull cutting wheels that slowly open a can of cat food while the cat yowls feline expletives are inexpensive and can be replaced with shiny new ones—often using only a screwdriver.

Between cleanings, watch out for paper or food getting caught in the drive-gear teeth. Such things caught here make the teeth slip, resulting in only a partially open can. Clean the teeth with a toothbrush and Red Juice also.

NOTE: Some small appliances mentioned in this chapter can't really be "maintained" because there's almost nothing that can be done in the way of maintenance—and when the thing breaks, it should be tossed away instead of being repaired. If you're tired of "throwaway" appliances, (re)consider replacing them with manual appliances. I'm very pleased with the manual can opener I've had since my last two-year-old, nonrepairable electric one croaked. My manual one is easy to use, easy to store (without taking up counter space twenty-four hours a day), and has a pleasing design, *and* I'm quite sure it will still be working decades from now. Also available are manual ice-cream makers, pasta makers, food mills, coffee grinders, and so forth.

Carpets and Rugs

Just like the floors they cover, carpets are susceptible to the plain old dirt carried onto them by shoes, feet, and paws, and blown onto them by gusts of wind through open windows. Plain old dirt is mostly pulverized specks of broken rock. Imagine a crushed-rock driveway reduced considerably in size, and you can visualize what destroys most carpets before their time. Proper maintenance starts with minimizing the crushed-rock effect by installing mats inside and outside all entryways to the house (see Rule 10). And vacuum, vacuum, vacuum. Several times a week is about right for active households, at least in areas of heavy use. Speaking of heavy use, don't install carpets in kitchens (visualize peanut butter toast facedown), patios (imagine a bowl of the chef's not-yet-world-famous BBQ sauce upside-down on the floor), bathrooms (mascara and Mercurochrome here and there), or garage—you get the idea. Rooms that get moisture or heavy traffic, or are too involved in food preparation, shouldn't be carpeted.

I'm fond of the saying "There are only two kinds of dirt in the world: the light kind that's attracted to dark objects, and the dark kind that's attracted to light objects." This is particularly apt for carpets. Avoid single-color dark or light carpets. Pick greens, rusts, and browns in midrange colors to reduce maintenance. Patterns and designs, multiple colors, multiple pile lengths, and varied textures all help disguise the inevitable and make maintenance easier. Whatever color, place the carpet on a quality pad to cushion and extend its life.

Vacuum the backs of small rugs at least yearly. Spot-clean as soon as a spot occurs—and if it's wet, clean it before it dries. Blotting up a little spill of coffee with a paper towel will remove it almost completely. Follow up with a quick spray with Red Juice and another good blotting, and it's *gone*. That same spill allowed to dry will be a permanent stain on some carpets. This is a good example of Rule 5. Much as you would prefer to sit quietly and drink your coffee instead of worrying about the small spill, do it now. Then pour yourself a fresh cup and start over again—or take it to work with you if you're now out of time. Get a good spot-removal kit and store it with your cleaning supplies.

Shampoo traffic areas as needed. This requirement is different from one household to another, but several times a year is not unusual. The best method for yearly deep cleaning is a shampoo followed immediately by extraction, but there are options for cleaning traffic areas. (1) Very small areas can be cleaned by hand. Mist Red Juice evenly on the dirty area—like a heavy morning dew. Now wipe the misted area with a cleaning cloth. Turn often. The surface dirt, along with the Red Juice, is absorbed into the cleaning cloth. (2) Dry cleaning: This method uses an absorbent powder or other material impregnated with a cleaner or solvent. Sprinkle the powder on the dirty area, agitate by machine or by hand with a brush, and vacuum it away. Several brands are available at grocery, hardware, and home-supply stores. (3) The same shampoo/extraction method used for deep cleaning.

Shampoo (deep-clean) the entire carpet only as needed. The Carpet and Rug Institute recommends deep cleaning every twelve to eighteen months depending on type, color, use, and the manufacturer's recommendations. In any event, no carpet-cleaning system gets out all stains and dirt, so keep up with the spot-cleaning and err on the side of shampooing a little too often rather than not often enough. Arrange carpet cleaning when you can keep dogs, cats, kids, spouses, and so on, off it until it is completely dry.

I recommend hiring a professional to do the deep cleaning. The money saved doing it yourself seems insignificant when you consider the cost of the machine, detergent, and prespotter, as well as picking up and dropping off the machine, moving and replacing furniture, and operating the machine. Professional equipment will routinely do a better job in a fraction of the time. And carpet cleaning can really take a toll on your aching back.

Change traffic patterns yearly, if possible, by rotating the rug. If you have wall-to-wall carpeting, rearrange furniture to change wear patterns.

Sun can damage carpets by fading the color and weakening the fibers. Protect with blinds (vertical ones, preferably), tinted windows, plants (vines), trellises, and so forth.

Stop any frays before the vacuum or something else turns them into a ruined carpet. Trim them with scissors or stitch them with a needle and thread—even if the job looks less than perfect. Or hire a professional for a more seamless job.

Position castors under furniture legs. Or attach furniture rests to the bottom of the legs of furniture that is moved often or that rests on hard floors such as wood or tile (see **Furniture**).

Sprayed-on soil retardants such as Scotchgard actually work, although they have to be reapplied after cleaning. If such a treatment is an option when you purchase a carpet, take it.

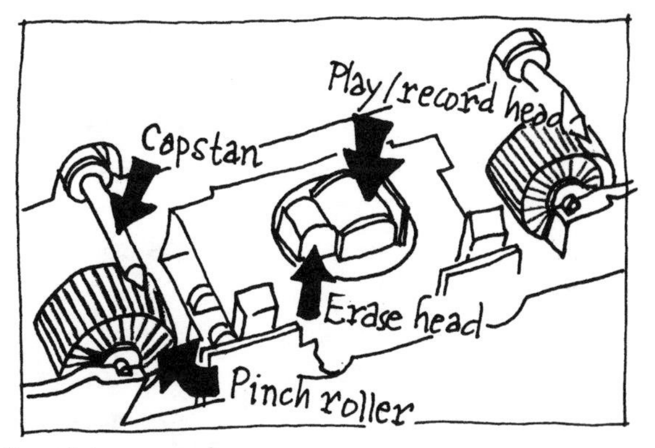

Cassette Tape Decks

Locate cassette players away from sunlight, heat, and the magnetic fields emitted by computers, TVs, and unshielded speakers. As with videocassettes, it's important to play clean audiocassettes in good condition to protect the drive mechanism and particularly the tape heads of the cassette deck.

Since an audio deck is a precision instrument with moving parts, the primary maintenance task is to keep these parts clean. The following should be cleaned on a regular basis (depending on use) or if they look dirty: play head, erase head, record head, pinch roller, capstan, and drive wheels. It's past time to clean if the tape keeps misfeeding, or if a loop or slack forms when you stop the tape, or if the sound quality becomes distorted during playback.

Unlike VCRs, many of the critical parts of audio decks are reasonably accessible. They fall into two main categories: metal and rubber. Almost everybody agrees on how to clean the former. Turn off the deck. Dampen a cotton swab with a bit of alcohol or head-cleaning fluid. Don't get it soaking wet or fluid will dribble where it shouldn't. Open the cassette door and wipe the metal parts listed on page 43 with the swab. No need to scrub hard: you're just trying to remove the layer of oxide, oils, and so on, that have accumulated. Rotate and check the tip of the swab often. If it keeps coming up brown or black, continue cleaning. Make sure strands of the cotton swab aren't left behind as you work.

Cleaning the rubber parts is a bit more controversial. Some sources recommend using alcohol as above, but others prefer using a specialized rubber cleaner (available at record stores or electronics stores). A compromise was offered by Keith Bianchi, who has seen audio trends come and go since 1953. He says alcohol can indeed attack rubber, but if you use only a dampened cotton swab for a brief period, you're probably not going to do any real harm. Whichever method you prefer, the next step is similar: Wipe the pinch rollers to remove the accumulated oxides and other gunk. The pinch rollers should be rather dull in appearance. If shiny, they need further cleaning. (This may seem contradictory, but the shininess consists of metal oxides that must removed to allow the dull rubber surface to "grab" the tape adequately.)

How often should you clean a deck? Authorities disagree wildly, and the answer also depends on such things as the type of tape you're using, the storage conditions, and even the type of metal used to make the heads. Recommendations vary from as little as every ten hours of use to every thirty hours. Trial and error is your best bet.

If you hear a constant noise during playback, or if high-frequency tones have dropped out so recordings sound dull, you might want to demagnetize the heads with a little gadget available at record and electronics stores. In general, you will probably have to demagnetize every second or third time you clean the heads.

Cassette Tapes

If you store audiocassettes properly, they will last for several decades. Take these simple steps to care for audiocassettes: Store them in a stable-temperature, moderately dry environment. Keep them in a plastic case to minimize dust accumulation. Store them on edge so they don't settle on the hub, which can lead to damaged tape edges. Audiophiles fast-forward and rewind tapes to release tension before recording. If a tape hasn't been played for a year, take it out for a spin by fast-forwarding or rewinding it to the other end. This will release accumulating tension and help prevent the transfer of the audio signal from one layer to the next (which results in a "pre-echo" often heard on older tapes).

If your tape deck is a low- or mid-priced model, audio pro Keith Bianchi notes that it probably will be happy only with Type I (iron oxide) tape, which happily is not only cheap but durable as well. The Type I industry favorite these days, hands-down, is TDK "D" formulation.

Cast-Iron Cooking Utensils

If they haven't already been seasoned, that's the first thing to do. First wash and scour with cleanser or fine steel wool. Rinse and dry thoroughly. Liberally coat the inside with vegetable oil and place on a burner at very low heat or in the oven at 250–300°F for two to three hours. Add more oil as needed. When finished, wipe off the extra oil and wash the utensil with dish soap and water. Rinse, and then dry first with a dish- or paper towel and then over a stove burner (a minute or less for a gas range or a few minutes for an electric range). Wash and dry in this manner after each use. Wipe with a thin coat of oil after several uses. To help prevent rust, once seasoned, store the utensil in a dry area without the lid in place. It shouldn't have to be reseasoned if properly maintained, but do so if it starts to look stained or rusty.

Ceramic Tile

These tiles are essentially glass, so protect them against chipping by using a cutting board in the kitchen and avoiding hard blows. Perseverance is the key to maintenance. Don't let floors or showers accumulate dirt, grease, mineral deposits, or soap scum. Even if you don't mind the unsavory appearance resulting from deferred cleaning, and even though the ceramic tile can be made like new again with liberal doses of elbow grease and household cleaner (one of ceramic tile's great advantages), the all-too-visible grout that's between the ceramic tiles is likely to become permanently stained without regular maintenance cleaning. That is, the tile will look great again, but the grout will not (see **Grout**).

Christmas Trees

These maintenance ideas come from the National Christmas Tree Association:

1. A tree should smell and look fresh. To test it, lightly grip a branch about six inches from its end and draw your hand to the branch tip, letting the needles slip through your fingers. Only a few needles should fall off. If the tree is small enough, you can pick it up and drop it on its cut end. Again, this should dislodge only a few needles.
2. Cut off a section of the tree's stem before placing it in water, and place the tree in water immediately afterward. It may drink a gallon of water in the first twenty-four hours, so check the water level often.

Cleaning Supplies

Maintaining your possessions with the wrong cleaner or cleaning tool can cause more damage than does regular use. If you've read our best seller on cleaning (*Speed Cleaning,* see Appendix B) you know that we have definite opinions about cleaning supplies based on our experience cleaning homes several hundred thousand times in San Francisco. Here are a few of the main time-saving strategies from *Speed Cleaning:*

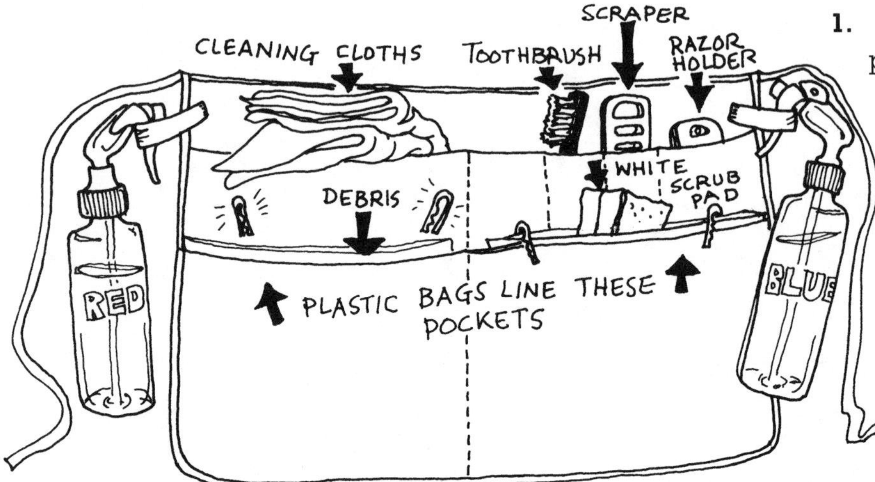

1. It's smarter to have only a few products that clean multiple surfaces rather than a different cleaner for each surface.

2. As important as cleaning *products* are, the *process* itself is equally important. We've found that many people rely rather heavily on "miracle" cleaners (many of which sit unused under the kitchen sink) because they don't know enough about the process.

3. The correct process starts with carrying your cleaning supplies with you in a cleaning apron to eliminate backtracking. When it comes to cleaning, it turns out to be easier (and faster) to work clockwise around a room once, cleaning from top to bottom and from back to front as you go. The alternative is to make fitful stops and starts and countless trips back and forth and up and down. You won't realize any substantial savings in time or effort unless you carry your supplies with you in a cleaning apron.

4. Carry a heavy-duty liquid cleaner (like Red Juice), a light-duty liquid or window cleaner (like Blue Juice), and a supply of white cotton cleaning cloths in your cleaning apron for most of the cleaning work. Add other products to your cleaning apron as needed, such as furniture polish and a polishing cloth for dusting, or a tile cleaner (like Tile Juice) when cleaning the bathroom. Red, Blue, and Tile Juice are what we call the actual products used and preferred by The Clean Team when we clean San Francisco homes. Some other basic supplies are: white scrub pad, whisk broom, tile brush, toilet brush, ostrich-down feather duster, toothbrush, razor in a holder, scraper, carryall tray, bleach, liquid cleanser, flat mop, clear ammonia, rubber gloves, and canister vacuum. You may add your own favorites to this list. Just remember to carry them with you in a cleaning apron or pocket so

you don't backtrack to retrieve them in the middle of the cleaning job. Depending on your home and floors, you may also need a dust mop and floor finish. (See Appendix A for further information and a list of comparable products.)

Closets

Maintenance of closets boils down to organization—a big, big subject—especially if all your closets are filled to the brim, not to mention overflowing drawers, a garage that's increasingly harder to fit the car into, and paper—articles, magazines, bills, junk mail, and so forth—spread throughout the house. Household organization solutions for closets and many other problem areas are discussed in our book *Clutter Control* (see Appendix B). In the meantime, remember to open the door to dust and vacuum inside closets as you do your regular housecleaning.

Coffeemakers

My brother tossed away his coffeepot when its water flow slowed to a trickle. I wonder how many others have done the same. Mineral and scale buildup made his pot slow to a crawl and its demise practically inevitable (which he could have avoided by using a water softener or distilled water). Besides the slowdown, the coffee also often tastes bitter. The buildup should be removed periodically.

Most coffeepot manufacturers sell a decalcifying agent, but a solution of half white vinegar and half water works fine. Pour the solution into the water reservoir and turn the pot on. Let half the solution drip into the carafe, shut off the coffeepot, and let stand for half an hour or so. Pour the solution back into the reservoir, turn on the coffeepot, and run the full amount of vinegar solution through the coffeepot. Do this several times (with fresh vinegar solutions) if you are treating a severe buildup. Finish up by rinsing all the accessible parts with water and then running plain water through a cycle. *Popular Mechanics* reports that at least some specialized coffeemaker cleaners work better—and *smell* better—than white vinegar.

Heated water passes through one or more small holes as it drips onto the coffee grounds. If the previous method didn't get the coffeepot up and running, it may be that hard-water deposits have completely closed these holes. If so, unplug and upend the coffeemaker to clean them out at least partially with a stiff wire or small nail. Now do the vinegar-and-water treatment just described to finish the job.

Coffee/Spice Grinders

When grinding, pulse the on/off switch rather than holding it down continuously. Don't run it for more than a minute or so without stopping to let it cool. And don't run it while empty or it will quickly overheat. If the switch needs cleaning, use a pastry brush along with a vacuum cleaner to deep-clean it. Use the same tools to clean out the grinder when changing from grinding coffee to grinding something else.

Compact Disc Players

Repair expert Daniel Bennett says there's little involved in caring for a CD player.

1. As with electronics in general, locate the player in a cool location. The player itself doesn't produce a lot of heat, but being kept cool helps ensure trouble-free operation.
2. CD players are sensitive to dust—especially smoky or greasy dust.
3. To avoid a variety of audio problems, double-check audio connections to be sure they are secure.

Even though CDs rely on very precise optical readings of incredibly small stored information, they are remarkably robust. Even portable and automotive units that are bounced all over the place usually don't need optical realignment. This is why, at least in part, extended warranties aren't necessary for CD players (along with most other things in the world). You can clean the optical laser lens, however, with one of the CD-cleaning discs now on the market. They have a fuzzy side that gently brushes the lens to remove accumulated dust.

Take the player in for service only when something goes wrong. Here are some symptoms that indicate it might be time to take yours to a professional to be cleaned or serviced: (1) audio noise, skipping, or sticking (make sure your discs are clean); (2) taking longer to start a disc or to complete a search; and (3) loading or starting a disc becomes erratic.

While a dirty videotape can harm a VCR, or a dirty record can ruin a stylus, it usually takes a cracked or broken CD to damage a CD player. Of course, dirty CDs may give rise to audio problems, so clean them according to the directions given under **Compact Discs,** discussed next.

Compact Discs

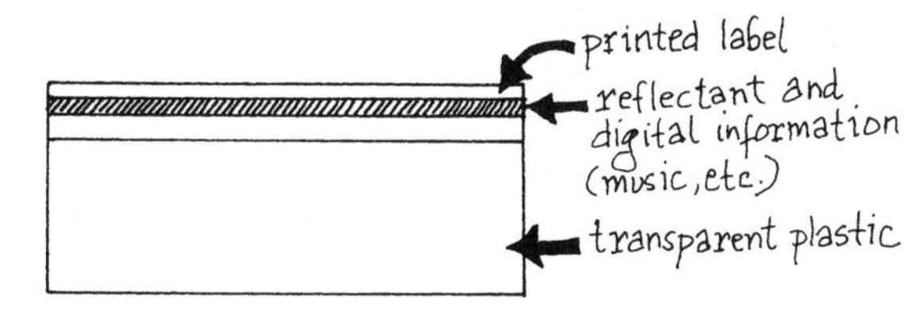

Compact disc cross section.

The data (music, images, or computer info) are stored on a reflective metal layer located below a protective coat of transparent plastic on the bottom (unpainted side) of the disc. Microscopic pits in the foil surface create the digital "ons" and "offs" that translate back into something intelligible when read by a laser focused on the foil surface.

The protective coat is quite durable, so the digital information is fairly safe from damage. If you're lucky, fingerprints or small scratches won't affect performance because the laser focuses on the metal layer below. Many fingerprints turn into a harmless blur, and the CD player can actually interpolate and fill in short breaks caused by scratches. CDs aren't indestructible, but good maintenance habits means they can last for decades. Hold them by the outside edge.

Wipe dirt and fingerprints with a clean soft cloth and CD-cleaning fluid or alcohol. Or wash gently with dish soap and water and dry with a soft clean cloth. It's safest to wipe from the center out (like spokes on a wheel), but as long as you're using a soft clean cloth and the proper fluid, you can wipe any way that's convenient without worry.

Keep the discs away from heat. CDs will warp if left in a dashboard player that can reach well above 125°F. And warps can cause the laser mechanism to fail prematurely by requiring it constantly to focus and refocus on the uneven surface at its extreme range.

NOTE: Many scratches that affect performance can be repaired. As long as the scratch didn't reach completely through the plastic layer to the foil layer, Compact Disc Repairman (see Appendix B) can mill the disc down by a few thousandths of an inch and then polish it back to its original smoothness. They claim that this process removes the scratches and allows the laser to read the disc as if it were new. It is undoubtedly less trouble and expense just to replace a damaged disc as long as copies are still available. Record stores also sell kits that will repair more minor scratches. Scratches from either side that are deep enough to reach the metal layer cannot be repaired.

Computers

Locate your computer and the monitor where they will remain relatively cool, dry, and dust-free, with plenty of room for air to circulate around each component. On particularly hot days, turn on a fan or air conditioner. Both the monitor and your eyes prefer subdued lighting. Don't put anything on the monitor that might block the ventilation grills on the top or rear.

At the risk of sounding preachy, I'm repeating the ubiquitous warning against leaving coffee, Budweiser, Diet Coke, or anything like it near the computer while you're surfing the Internet. If you do this five hundred times, it's bound to spill at least once and ruin the keyboard or other components.

A few lights or an electric clock won't matter, but don't plug the computer into a circuit shared with a space heater, for example.

Besides installing a UL-rated surge protector to protect against electrical surges, it's wise to unplug your computer in the event of an impending thunderstorm. Also unplug the phone line to the modem. It's also prudent to unplug or at least turn off the computer if the weather is such that a power interruption is likely. If you don't, when the power resumes all sorts of electrical aberrations can occur that you do *not* want your computer to experience.

If you're serious about computing, or if you are the frequent victim of blackouts, brownouts, surges, and electric storms, you might consider investing in an uninterruptible power supply (UPS). It's essentially a constantly charging battery that activates in a fraction of a second to provide power to your computer when normal power fails. If the power goes down, it will sound an alarm and keep your computer and peripheral devices up and running for several minutes—long enough for you to save your work and shut down the system in an orderly fashion. The UPS is usually connected to everything but the printer (which draws too much power for the UPS to sustain for long).

Dust is another enemy. Cover components when not in use. Wipe ventilation slots with a cloth, or gently vacuum them. If you remove the computer case, use a can of compressed air to remove accumulated dust from inside the computer. Clean the keyboard with the brush attachment of a vacuum cleaner when you do your regular housecleaning. Or use a can of compressed air, but protect yourself and other things in the area from flying dust. Also carefully vacuum out the printer to remove bits of paper and dust that have settled in it. Clean the monitor with a cleaning cloth sprayed with Blue Juice.

Keep unshielded speakers (i.e., the magnets inside them) plus any other magnets and electric motors away from the monitor. If the monitor becomes magnetized, it will display weird fluorescent colors and may even need degaussing (demagnetizing). Nearby power lines can also cause noticeable monitor interference—even electric wiring in the wall or behind the wall. Don't move your computer while it's on. The hard drive is particularly vulnerable. Finally, diskettes stored upright are less prone to accidental damage.

Computer Mouse. Under the theory that the more the part is moving, the more trouble it will cause, the computer mouse is one of those components that will require relatively more care over time. The main preventive step you can take is not to run it across dusty and gritty surfaces, where it will pick up and transport the grit and dust into its interior with great ease. In other words, *do* use a mouse pad rather than the desk surface, and keep the pad dusted and cleaned.

If your mouse starts to freeze up or work erratically, it's time to clean it. With the computer off and/or the mouse disconnected, flip it over on its back and remove the cover plate that keeps the mouse ball in place. It will either twist or slide off. The ball can then be tipped out to clean. Don't use a strong solvent or ammonia: a plain damp cloth or one lightly sprayed with Red Juice should work just fine. Set it aside to dry.

Then turn your attention to the metal rollers in the mouse housing that are spun by the ball. Wipe them with a cotton swab barely dampened with alcohol. If you have a can of air handy, it wouldn't hurt to give the area a blast or two. Then replace the ball and cover, wipe off any grungy fingerprints on the top, and your mouse is on its way again.

Convection Ovens

Like so many other things around the house, perhaps yourself included, the oven needs to vent. Leave a few inches of space around and over the oven for this purpose. Inside, make sure there's at least an inch clearance between the food being cooked and the sides, top, and bottom of the oven. Clean any filters in front of the fan every few months or as needed. Wash them in soapy water and allow them to dry before reinstalling. Clean the fan itself and the interior of the oven with Red Juice, and wipe with a cleaning cloth.

Countertops

Whether your counter is made from tile, Formica, Corian, or marble, and no matter what the salesperson told you, protect it from hot pots, pans, or baking dishes taken directly from the stove or oven. Also, don't cut food on it. The countertop and/or the knife will be damaged. Liquids have a way of eventually getting to places where they cause great damage, so wipe up spills, including plain water, as soon as they occur.

Crystal Display Pieces

Crystal in all shapes and sizes, including crystal or glass sculptures, has some important maintenance considerations:

1. Surface protectors for crystal display pieces (such as vases, bowls, and sculptures) are doubly important because they protect the surface below, as well as the piece itself. Use self-adhesive felt pads.
2. Wash by hand only. For smaller pieces, use a rubber mat in the sink. Since diamonds cut glass, remove any diamond rings you may be wearing. Use warm water and regular dish soap (ammonia can start to remove gold rims). Don't lift pieces out of the water to wash them. Wash under water where if you drop it, it probably won't break. Dry

by hand with a clean cotton towel. Clean larger pieces with a cleaning cloth and Blue Juice. Spray the cloth and wipe the piece clean and dry.

3. Use both hands when moving or using crystal. I once owned a crystal water pitcher that broke when it was lifted by its handle. I should have supported it with a second hand.
4. Change water every other day in small-necked vases, and every day in large-necked vases or bowls of flowers. Remove lines left by evaporated water with a solution of half water and half white vinegar. Fill the vase with the solution past the lines and allow it to sit for several hours or overnight. Use a bottle brush to agitate, discard the solution, and wash normally.
5. Heat or cold can crack crystal. Don't let candles burn too low in a crystal candleholder. Prefill a crystal ice bucket with cold water. It's wise to avoid refrigerating or microwaving crystal pieces.

Curtains and Drapes

They take a beating from the sun and will eventually be ruined by its effects. Delay the inevitable by protecting them with awnings, outdoor trees or other plants, window film or tint, or similar tactics. (The same applies to furniture and other light-sensitive possessions.) Vacuum the tops of curtains and drapes monthly. Vacuum the rest of them yearly.

Dehumidifiers

A dehumidifier is an air conditioner that doesn't cool. Maintenance is therefore very similar to an air conditioner's. Vacuum the evaporator coils once or twice a year with the brush attachment. If necessary, use Red Juice and a toothbrush to remove grime, and spray with water to rinse.

Don't let water stagnate in the water container or run over into the base of the unit. Empty the water container daily. Wash it with soap and water, and allow it to air-dry (or put it in the dishwasher if it's safe to do so).

Wash or replace the filter once a month.

Dishwashers

Maintenance starts with correct usage. Scrape or rinse pieces of food off dishes and cookware. No matter what the salesperson or the TV commercial told you about not having to rinse or scrape, no dishwasher can successfully flush away a lot of food. Most can deal with only small amounts of undried soft food. And although some foods can be successfully removed by the dishwasher, they may discolor other items beings washed or the inside of the dishwasher itself. Among the chief culprits are mayonnaise, mustard, and catsup. All things considered, it's best to give a quick rinse or wipe to most dishes as you load the dishwasher. The disposer (or the garbage can) can deal with solid food a lot easier than the dishwasher's drainage system can.

Load the dishwasher in such a way that dishes and cookware face the center where the strongest water sprays can reach them. Place knives and other sharp or heavy items with care so they don't cut the protective covering of the dishwasher racks. Once these are cut, rust will develop shortly. Glasses should be placed between prongs, not over them. Don't block the spray arm or spray tower.

Appliance expert Al Hale advises running the dishwasher once a week empty of dishes and soap, but with a half cup or so of nonsudsing ammonia or white vinegar added instead. This treatment can remove and help prevent a film buildup that inevitably arises as residual dirt and grease are deposited on interior surfaces during everyday use. Wait until the water is being pumped into the machine, then open the door and pour in the vinegar or ammonia (but not both!) onto the floor of the machine. If the interior is stained because of hard water, run the empty dishwasher with two cups or more of white vinegar as just described.

If your plumbing system has hard water, you'll get better performance if you regularly use a liquid rinse agent. (Look for it in grocery stores in the same area as dishwasher soap.) It's added to the dishwasher's dispenser for rinse agents, usually located next to the dishwasher's soap dispenser.

But don't use a rinse agent if the water is naturally soft or if you have a water softener.

Keep the pump screens free of small food particles and other deposits. The pump screens are usually located in the well at the base of the unit. Some units don't have screens, so if you don't see an obvious opening in the bottom of the dishwasher with a screen on it, don't worry about it. It doesn't have one. If it does, check for large food particles. Remove them and then scrub the screen with a toothbrush.

It's possible that the holes in the rotating spray arms, especially the lower ones, are clogged with food particles. Using a paper clip, pin, or thin wire, try to get under food particles and *pull* them out through the hole rather than pushing them back in the hole where they will reclog as soon as you run the dishwasher. (Both the pump screen and spray-arm holes should stay clear and unplugged if you rinse and load as described on page 62.)

The dishwasher requires fairly hot water (around 140°F). If you're in doubt, check the water temperature with a candy or meat thermometer. Allow the dishwasher to run through one fill-and-pump cycle and let the dishwasher fill with water a second time. Then unlatch the door and slowly open it. Remove the silverware basket and place the thermometer in the water toward the middle of the tub. Don't rest the thermometer on the floor of the dishwasher or you'll get a false reading. If the temperature isn't between 120° and 140°F, you will not get good washing results. Hot water is essential for dissolving grease and activating detergents. Raise the temperature setting of the water heater and retest (see **Water Heaters**). If this doesn't result in a higher temperature at the dishwasher, or if the water heater is already set at a high enough temperature, have the heating element of the dishwasher checked. (Not all dishwashers have one, but a heating element is designed to boost the temperature of the hot water delivered from the house's water heater.)

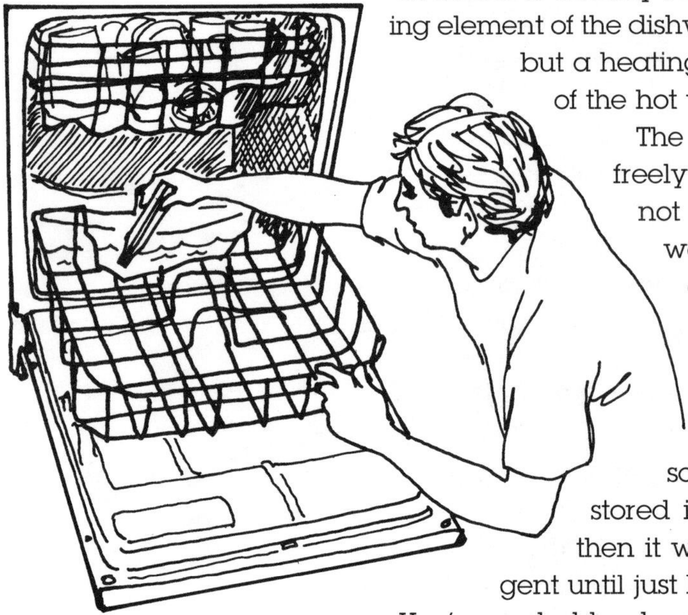

The detergent dispenser must open and close freely. If detergent builds up here, the dispenser will not open and close on schedule and the dishes won't get clean. Remove any leftover soap. Then clean thoroughly with Red Juice and a toothbrush. Rinse and wipe dry. And naturally, when running the dishwasher, use only detergent made for dishwashers, and don't use it if it's "lumpy." It gets that way fairly quickly, sometimes within a week or two (especially if stored in a damp location, like under the sink), and then it won't dissolve during use. Also, don't add detergent until just before you're ready to run the machine.

You've probably already figured out that you don't need the heat cycle to dry the dishes. The dishes get almost completely dry without it. Not using it means less chance of a breakdown, and you'll cut down the electric bill as well.

By the way, if you see a puddle of water at the bottom of the dishwasher after use, don't worry. It's standard procedure for water to be left there at the end of its cycle.

Doors and Door Hardware

Exterior doors are a particularly expensive and important part of your home. One of the most important steps to ensure their long-term health is obvious, but it happens often enough that it bears stating: Don't slam them. They will crack. They will stick or be difficult to close. Stucco walls will crack. Hinges will loosen, locks and doorjambs will fail.

Paint wooden doors every four to six years. Use a fungicide additive if mildew is a problem. Varnished doors may have to be recoated more often. Remember that doors have six sides, and each one needs equal protection by paint or varnish.

Keep doorknobs, locks, and hinges operating smoothly and quietly. Once a year or two, use graphite powder or Teflon spray (e.g., Tri-Flow or Borden's) for locks and doorknobs. Graphite comes in a small squeezable plastic bottle that allows you to apply it into tight spots. Although it's usu-

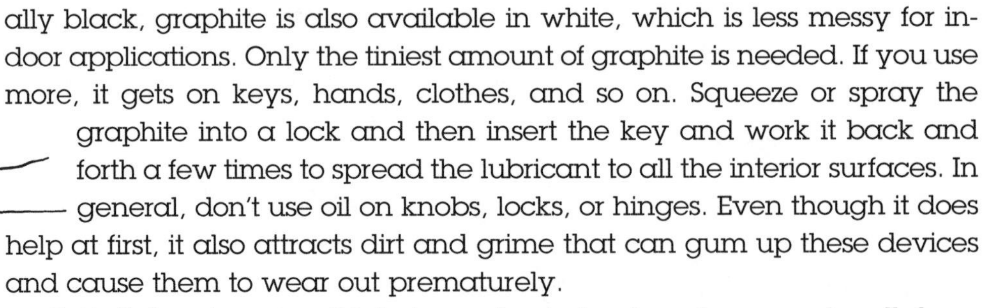

ally black, graphite is also available in white, which is less messy for indoor applications. Only the tiniest amount of graphite is needed. If you use more, it gets on keys, hands, clothes, and so on. Squeeze or spray the graphite into a lock and then insert the key and work it back and forth a few times to spread the lubricant to all the interior surfaces. In general, don't use oil on knobs, locks, or hinges. Even though it does help at first, it also attracts dirt and grime that can gum up these devices and cause them to wear out prematurely.

Install doorstops on all interior and exterior doors to prevent wall damage from doorknobs. If the bottom of the door isn't suitable for a doorstop, install it at the top. If a door handle still touches the wall, even with a doorstop on the bottom, put another doorstop at the top of the door. If you don't like doorstops, use a pair of hinge stops. They attach directly to the hinge pins and are less noticeable (if you are one of the few people who notices doorstops at all).

You might consider removing extra interior doors. Our home in San Francisco had doors between the hall and the living room and between the kitchen and the dining room. Neither door had been closed for five years, so I put them in the garage. We have saved time dusting and vacuuming ever since, and we now have more space in each room.

Sliding doors usually get more and more difficult to operate. Clean the runners as needed with a vacuum, then with a toothbrush, Red

Juice, and a cleaning cloth. Check to be sure weep holes are open. Then apply Teflon spray or other lubricant and the door should slide easily again.

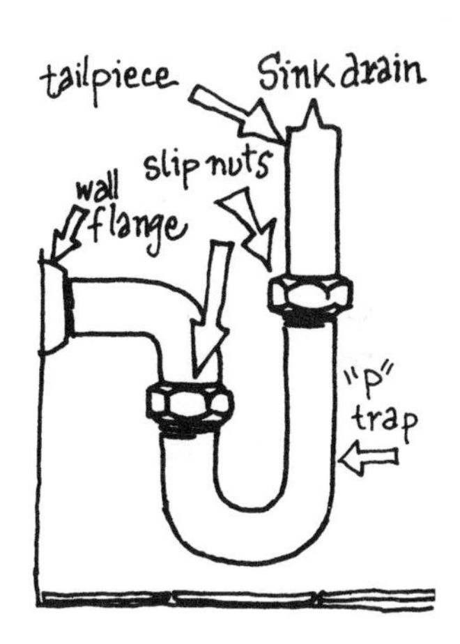

Drains

A sink, shower, or toilet drain is shaped to create a "trap" that holds water and forms a barrier or seal against sewer odors and gas that would otherwise enter the house from the drainage system. It is commonly called a "P-trap." A brilliant invention, actually: a fully functional seal with no moving parts. Infrequently used drains such as those serving a spare shower or basement sink should be refilled by turning on the water briefly to replace evaporated water and to ensure that the water barrier is in place.

Because of their shape, drains are highly susceptible to clogs. I've had people tell me they were actually surprised that cotton swabs and matches clog drains. Other obvious examples of things that don't belong in drains include—but are not limited to—grease, oil, hair, and any paper other than toilet paper. The list includes practically everything you can name besides waste water.

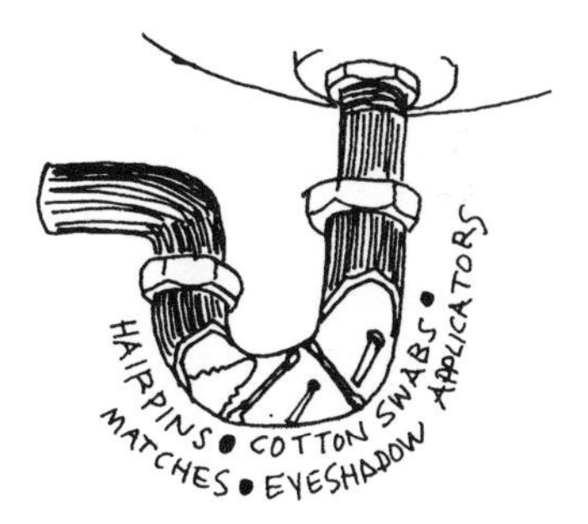

Plunger Use. Next to prevention, the best approach for clearing a clogged drain is still the venerable plunger. Here's how to use one:

1. Plug any sink overflow vent with a wet cloth. If it's a double sink, close or plug the other drain. It's best to have a helper hold the wet cloth firmly in place.

2. The plunger's rubber cup must cover the drain opening completely, and standing water must cover the cup's edge halfway or so up its side. Add water if necessary, but remove extra water to avoid giving yourself a splash bath. Use a cup or a bucket to remove all but two to three inches of standing water. Tilt the plunger so most of the air under it can escape as you put it into position.

3. Work the plunger up and down fifteen to twenty times. This method builds up the pressure needed to break the clog loose. You can increase its ability to build up pressure by smearing a little petroleum jelly on the rim of the plunger. Repeat the sequence several times.

4. If the water starts to slowly trickle out, take a break while it does and then refill with hot—better yet, boiling—water, let it drain out, and try it again with the plunger.

If this procedure has been unsuccessful, the next step might be one of the following: renting a plumber's snake, removing the P-trap itself, or calling a plumber. The snake is fraught with difficulties, as it's quite easy to poke it through the surprisingly thin wall of a drainpipe (especially after a few years of corrosion). And it can be surprisingly difficult to reassemble the drainpipes properly. Unfortunately, this is one of those problems that may not have a simple solution. A pipe can be filled with debris all the way to the sewer or septic tank, or it may be so badly invaded by roots or grease that it has to be replaced. You may also have to start a maintenance schedule with a rooter company. My personal recommendation is to call a plumber.

Some drains are old and corroded or installed so close to level (instead of downhill) that they clog fairly regularly despite your good habits. Further maintenance is required. There is great disagreement whether it's okay to dump lye-based drain cleaners into the drain once a week or even once a month. On one hand, if you ask almost any consumer advocate, these drain cleaners are toxic chemicals, they eat into pipes, and they destroy beneficial bacteria in a septic system. If you ask the manufacturer, they are quite safe if used according to directions.

Well, they do contain dangerous chemicals *and* they are effective when used as a maintenance aid to keep a sluggish drain working. I have used them that way in an old house in San Francisco with very touchy drains. However, you can keep a prone-to-clog drain open just as well by pouring boiling water (a half gallon or so) into it once a week, once a month, or according to what you have learned about the drain (i.e., before it clogs). Follow up in ten minutes or so with a minute or two of hot water from the tap.

Enzyme drain cleaners are effective and safe, but are rather slow-acting. Therefore, they aren't good for emergencies but are fine as maintenance. Use these when you go on vacation or can otherwise take the time necessary to let the enzyme cleaner work, as some of them take overnight to work. One caution: They are not usually very effective on hair.

Dryers

The complete and unrestricted venting of hot, moist air from a dryer is critical to its operation, its long life, and your safety. Therefore, the single most important maintenance step is keep the lint screen clean. So, just like the directions always say, clean the lint screen after each use. In fact, if you are drying a very linty load, clean the lint screen partway through the drying cycle. Whenever the screen is clogged, the dryer will run longer. It can be working at less than half its normal efficiency, so it costs that much more to operate and it will wear out that much more quickly. Also keep the lint screen in good condition. If it is bent, punctured, rusted, or no longer fits properly, replace it.

The antistatic sheets that are tossed into the dryer by many of us with each load may not be such a good idea, according to appliance guru Al Hale. If they lodge in the lint screen, they will block the flow of air just as if you hadn't cleaned the lint screen to begin with.

Every few months, remove the lint screen and vacuum behind it to get at the lint that manages to sneak behind the lint screen. Poke the vacuum hose (with or without the crevice tool) to remove as much lint as you can.

Check and clean, if necessary, the vent duct once a year by disconnecting it from the back of the dryer. Also, the duct should have no sags, which can trap water, or sharp turns, which can trap lint. Make sure the duct was not squished (even partially) when the dryer was pushed into place. Any obstruction can build up heat within the duct and can shorten the life of your dryer. Vinyl ducts have been known to catch fire, so when it's time to replace yours, change to a flexible aluminum one. In many cities, aluminum ducts are now required by code for new and retrofit construction.

Finish the inspection of the dryer by checking the far end of the duct at the exhaust hood once a year. Make sure that air can flow freely out of it and that the vent flap opens and closes properly. You should be able to feel a strong exhaust when the dryer is operating. Birds, spiders, and other unwelcome housemates can try to make their home here but should be encouraged to relocate. Also, lint can build up within this hood. Check with a flashlight and remove any accumulation with a screwdriver or similar device. If there is *not* a strong exhaust, remove the vent cover to investigate. If you don't find anything, go inside the house and pull the dryer away from the wall to get at the near end of the duct. Disconnect the vent duct from the dryer and from the exhaust port (where the vent duct attaches to the wall or floor). Clean the duct by first vacuuming what you can. Then take it outside and flush thoroughly with water and hang it up fully extended to dry. If yours is a rigid metal duct in sections, separate the sections and clean inside each section with the vacuum and the brush attachment or with a long-handled brush. Use the crevice tool to vacuum into the dryer and into the exhaust port as far as you can. Clean the floor and vacuum the back of the dryer with the brush attachment. Before you move the dryer back into position, reattach the exhaust duct and recheck the exhaust volume. If it's still weak, call for service.

It may help motivate you to inspect the dryer's venting pathways and to clean the vent screen after each use by observing that lint is extremely flammable. The instant it can't get out, a potentially dangerous situation arises. Likewise, don't vent the dryer underneath the house. Lint accumulating in the crawl space, attic, or basement is highly flammable.

The soap, pretreatment agents, chlorine bleach, ammonia, rust removers, and so forth that can corrode a washer's surface can do the same thing to a dryer. Some of these products will corrode both the painted surface and the plastic controls as well. Wipe up such spills promptly and try not to use the dryer as a work top. Just use a sink instead of the dryer (or washer) top, and quickly rinse the sink after use.

Overloading also wears out the dryer before its time. Besides, your clothes will dry faster and will emerge with fewer wrinkles if you give them some breathing room in the dryer.

Dust

If you're interested in lowering maintenance in the house by reducing the overall amount of dust, here are some subjects to check on:

1. Filters (see **Heating and Cooling Systems**).
2. Effective floor mats (see Rule 10).
3. Weather-stripping around **Doors** and **Windows.**
4. Lint from your **Dryer.**

Electrical Maintenance

Ground-Fault Circuit Interrupters (GFIs or GFCIs). You probably have this type of electrical device in your kitchen, bathroom, basement, pool area, deck, or anyplace where water is likely to be present. GFIs detect a

short circuit (caused by water or any other reason) and will shut down the circuit within a fraction of a second—faster than electrical current can travel to your heart, where it poses its greatest danger. A fuse or circuit breaker protects the house's wiring. A GFI protects *you.*

The manufacturers request that you test GFIs once a month. This is easy enough to accomplish, as there is a test button right in the middle of it. Push it. You'll hear a little click, and the circuit will be interrupted. Push the reset button to restore power to the outlet or circuit. I don't expect to live long enough to meet the person who actually does this every month.

Overloaded Circuits. If you have a circuit that regularly trips the breaker or blows a fuse, find out if it's due to an overload. If it's not, call an electrician. Ignoring it could result in a fire. And even if it is an overload, unless you solve the problem by redistributing the appliances that are plugged into that circuit, you may want to talk to an electrician to learn whether additional capacity is needed.

Electronics

(Also see individual components—**Compact Disc Players, TVs,** etc.)

Allowing unhampered air circulation through all vents is critical to avoid overheating. The rubber feet under most electronic devices provide the minimum gap between adjoining units, so don't remove them or defeat their purpose by setting the unit on carpeting. It's also smart to keep cabinet or closet doors open when using the components inside. Vacuum the vent openings occasionally to keep dust from clogging them. Keep electronics away from open windows, high heat, and the cat.

Naturally, electronic gear will stay cleaner longer if you cover it when not in use. If you do spill something on one, turn it off, unplug it, turn it over, and wipe it to remove what you can. Then wait a few days before you plug it back in. If it works, fine. If not, it's usually smarter to start shopping rather than take it in for repair.

If you have invested a great deal in the equipment, proper maintenance includes having a lightning arrester professionally installed. Connect the equipment to its own ("dedicated") electrical circuit, and install a rated surge protector as well.

Here's a bit of useful information from Sony Hawaii (see Appendix B). Not using a unit for a long period could cause premature component failure. An electronic unit should be used once a month or so to help ensure that it stays in proper working condition. Turning it on will electrically energize the components, which in turn can help prevent premature failure. Ordinarily, electronic components should last for about five thousand hours of use. But you can't quit using something for years and still expect it to work—or at least to last five thousand hours. So it's counterproductive to store electronic equipment for the sake of prolonging its life.

Fans

Box and Oscillating Fans. Clean the blades when you can see dirt, as an accumulation can unbalance the blades and wear out bearings. Clean them with a vacuum, or disassemble the fan and wipe with Red Juice and a cleaning cloth. Align blades (metal ones only) by measuring and bending into position as needed. The motor shaft in unsealed motors should be lubricated with lightweight machine oil once a year or so.

Ceiling Fans. Whenever you find yourself cleaning a fan (which we recommend you do about once a year), check that the fan is still tight and not working its way loose from the ceiling mounting. Constant vibration when running and/or from a pull-chain switch can eventually loosen the entire fan. Check that fan blades are tight also. Blades should turn freely with the power off. If they don't, have the fan serviced.

You can stretch the period of time between cleanings by purchasing a

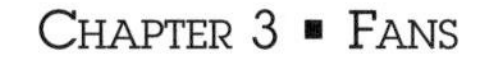

specialized duster for ceiling fans. The one we use is called a rabbit-ear duster. It bends to fit around the fan and remove dust better. However, until they invent a brake to keep the fan blades stationary during the dusting operation, cleaning attempts will be only partially successful—even with the right tool.

If the fan starts to wobble when running, the most likely cause is that a balance weight has fallen off. The next most likely cause is that it needs an additional balance weight. The solution in either case is to add a balance weight. First try to eliminate other possibilities:

1. Take a good look from below to make sure no blades or blade holders are askew.
2. Check that the screws through the blades into the blade holders are tight.
3. Check that all blade holders are tightly attached to the flywheel.
4. Check that all blades are equidistant from the ceiling.

If the fan is askew or if the blades aren't level with the ceiling, have it serviced. If none of these things are the problem, here are the steps to determine where to place a balance weight. (Most manufacturers provide a blade-balancing kit. Excavate yours from the tool cabinet or purchase a new one.)

1. Select one blade and place a balance clip midway on the blade on the rear edge. (A balance clip is part of the manufacturer's balancing kit. If you do not have this kit, use a medium-size metal washer, and tape it in place.)
2. Start the fan. Note whether the wobble is better or worse. Stop the fan and repeat on each blade noting the blade on which the greatest improvement is achieved.
3. Select the blade that gave the greatest improvement and move the clip outward or inward on this blade. Test each to find the position where the clip gives the greatest improvement.
4. Remove the clip and install a balancing weight on the top and in the center of the blade near the point where the clip was positioned. (If you don't have a balancing weight, firmly tape the washer in place.)
5. If the wobble is not completely gone, you can start over again and apply additional weights.

Two cautions should be mentioned. Allow the blades to stop between each test. It's easy to get impatient and reach up too soon. Either the balance clip or the metal washer could fly off if not secure.

Exhaust or Vent Fans. Ceiling or wall exhaust fans in the kitchen and bathroom eventually get grungy—even if you vacuum or brush their grills regularly. When there is a visible buildup (or once a year if you can't see into the unit) remove the grill by removing the screws that hold it in place. (First turn off the power and ensure it can't be turned on accidentally by flipping the circuit, removing the fuse, or taping the power switch off.) Put the grill and filter, if any, into the dishwasher or soak in dish soap and hot water in the sink. Replace the filter after it's been washed a few times. Use the crevice tool to clean the housing and a Red Juice–dampened cloth to clean the fan blades. Reassemble.

Faucets

Leaky faucets do more than merely waste water. If the hot-water faucet leaks only one drop per second, it means paying monthly for two hundred gallons of hot water from which you received no soothing hot bath. A little trickle is more like six thousand gallons a month—a waste of precious resources as well as money. Besides, if it's hard water, some of it undoubtedly will evaporate and leave tenacious or even permanent mineral deposits and/or stains.

Washers. Usually it is a worn washer that's causing the drip. If the faucet has no washers, it is probably a cartridge type. The latter lasts longer but still must be serviced periodically. Learn how to replace either one. This isn't quite a fix-it; I prefer to call it maintenance when the alternative is to call in a $70/hour plumber to install a fifteen-cent washer.

Here are some very basic how-to-change-a-washer instructions. Because of the subject of this book, there's a lot of ground that we're not covering. (And there are any number of excellent home-improvement books that cover the subject in great detail.) But we want to give you the basic idea and a dose of encouragement so you can see that the task is not insurmountable. If you feel reasonably comfortable that you could tackle disassembly of a faucet—armed with a screwdriver, adjustable wrench, and a pair of pliers—we'll help you get it back together again (sans drip).

1. Determine that a store with *everything* you may need is wide-open. Make sure that it will still be open if you are delayed or if the project

takes longer than expected (practically a certainty, at least the first time).

2. Turn the water supply to the faucet off, and open the faucet to drain the line. **Note:** If the faucet doesn't have a shut-off valve under the sink, or if the faucet is very old, or if it's a shower faucet in a wall—for heaven's sake put your feet up, call a plumber, and turn on *Oprah* instead. You'll live longer. It's just too likely that something will go wrong that costs more than the fifteen-cent washer.

3. As you disassemble the parts, place them on the counter in the precise order in which you removed them. Always take worn parts to the store for exact replacements. If in the slightest doubt, make yourself a diagram or Polaroid shot and then take everything to the store. Also, make a note of the manufacturer's name if it's not clearly shown on the part.

4. Put a stopper in the sink. Otherwise, the very first thing that pops loose will head for the drain. (This is not a superstition; the drain is, after all, the lowest point in the sink.) Also place a towel over the sink to protect it from scratches. The next few steps will diverge a bit, depending on whether the faucet has a separate handle for hot and cold or is one of the newer faucets (ball, cartridge, or disc) that has a single pivoting handle. The following instructions are for conventional faucets unless otherwise noted.

5. Remove the handle. Many faucets have a decorative cap that can be removed by prying it off with a screwdriver or knife. Then remove the screw keeping the handle in place. For single-handled faucets, the setscrew underneath the faucet handle must be unscrewed before the handle itself can be removed.

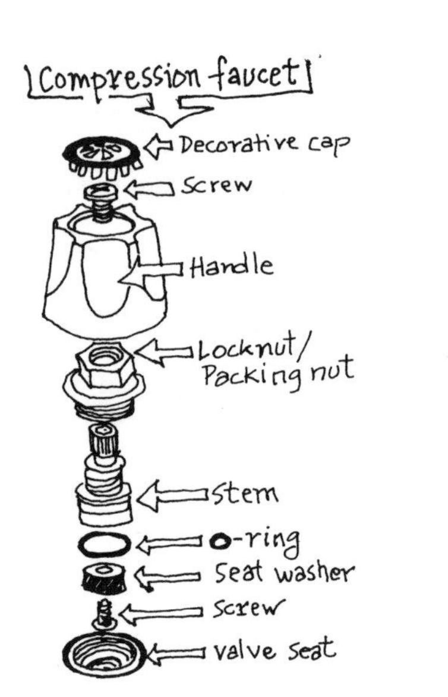

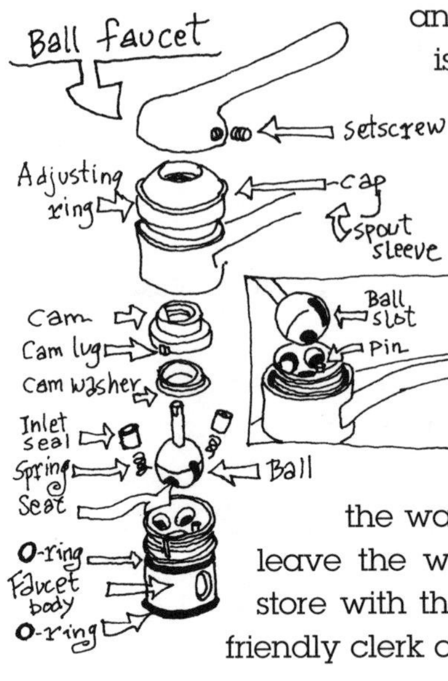

6. Remove the packing (or bonnet) nut with an adjustable wrench. Especially if this nut is tight, hold on to the faucet for dear life with one hand as you turn the wrench with the other. To avoid scratching visible parts (and even chrome scratches rather easily) wrap the faucet with tape or a cloth.

7. Unscrew the faucet stem by hand. The washer is located at its far end, held in place by another screw. If the stem looks like it's in good condition, remove the washer and replace it. If the stem looks worn, leave the washer alone and get thee to a hardware store with the whole assembly (stem and washer). The friendly clerk at the hardware store is much more likely to

remain friendly if you do so. Some washers are flat, and others are beveled. The clerk will be able to make more sense of the whole affair if you bring in the worn stem and washer together. For single-handled ball faucets, remove and replace the rubber seat and spring; remove the faucet spout; remove and replace the O-rings. For cartridge faucets, replace the cartridge. The same friendly clerk will help you select replacement parts.

8. Screw the faucet stem back in (but not too tightly). Replace the packing nut. For a single-handled faucet, replace the ball assembly as well as the spout.

9. Turn the water supply back on. Check for leaks. Adjust the packing nut as needed. Finally, replace the handle.

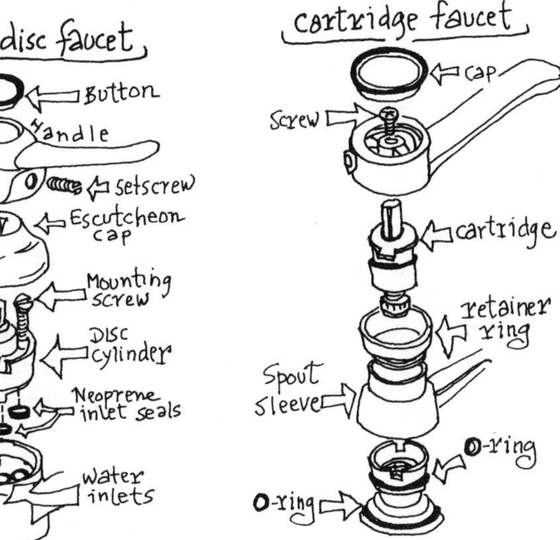

If you happen to be home while a plumber is installing a new faucet, ask him or her how to replace the washer. Also ask if you can buy a spare washer or two. If you're also willing to change the P-trap (see **Drains**), ask to buy one or two of them and ask for a short demo of how to replace it. According to expert plumber Jeff Meehan, the only types of P-trap that will really last are 17-gauge brass or ABS or PVC plastic.

While you have his or her attention, why not ask for recommendations on draining or flushing your water heater (see **Water Heaters**) or whether or not the plumber offers a regular maintenance agreement?

Don't clean faucets (or anything else you don't want to get scratched) with a green pad. The green pad removes a layer of chrome or brass along with the dirt each time you clean.

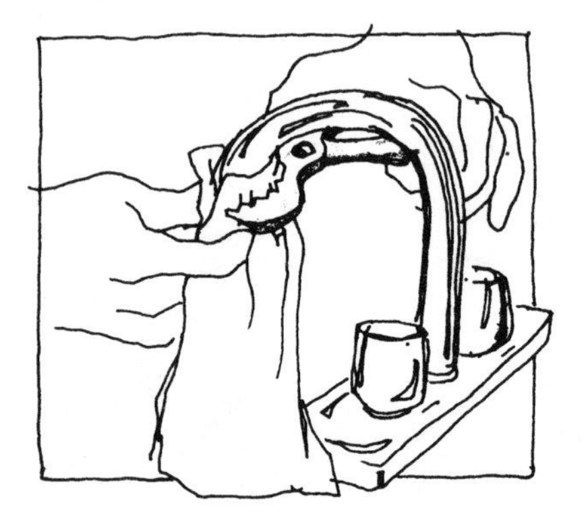

Aerators. Found in kitchen and bathroom faucets, aerators add air to water to reduce splashing. As debris works its way through the water line, it will get trapped behind the aerator and restrict the flow of water. Unscrew it from the mouth of the faucet. Use a pair of pliers and a cleaning cloth or piece of tape wrapped around the aerator to keep it from being scratched. Rinse the filter and washer, replace them in their original order, and screw the aerator back on the faucet. You will learn how often this has to be done, but the most obvious sign is that the flow of water is reduced or misdirected.

If the deposits in the aerator filter don't rinse off, they are probably hard-water deposits. To remove these deposits, soak the disassembled aerator overnight in a solution of equal parts water and white vinegar.

Fax Machines

Go over the keypad with the brush attachment of a vacuum cleaner as you do your routine vacuuming. Find out (from the owner's manual) where the glass is that covers the scanner portion of the fax, and clean it once a year or more with alcohol and a cotton swab.

Fire Extinguishers

Recharge or replace the unit if it's low. That's the easy part. Manufacturers recommend checking the pressure monthly. The hard part is remembering to do it—and remembering where the extinguishers all are. If you have trouble doing so, create a maintenance schedule book and add fire extinguishers to the list, or add a monthly entry to your calendar or daily planning book. It's too important to take the chance that you might forget. Locate extinguishers in a visible—or at least very accessible—place, which will make it all that easier to check on their pressure as you do your routine cleaning. Exhume them from the back of cupboards and out from under the garage workbench, where they have been buried for years. And don't allow clutter to displace the fire extinguishers over time.

Take the time to make sure that other family members know where the extinguishers are. It doesn't help much in an emergency if you're the only one who knows where to find the extinguishers and you don't happen to be home.

Also give a lesson to family members on how and when to use a fire extinguisher. They are a quick defense against small home fires only. Teach youngsters to call 911 first. Most home extinguishers are rated multipurpose (ABC), which means they can fight all classes of household fires: A is for extinguishing trash, wood, and paper; B liquids and grease; and C electrical equipment. To use a fire extinguisher, pull the pin or other release mechanism and aim at the *base* of the fire. Squeeze the handle and sweep from side to side until the fire is out. You should always have an escape route available if the fire gets out of hand. Also be alert that extinguished fires don't flare back up.

Fireplaces

Call in a professional chimney sweep after two or three years of use in a new home and before the first year's use in a used home. He or she can clean the chimney, if needed, and advise you on how often cleaning should be repeated.

If your chimney doesn't have a chimney cap, have one installed. It protects the interior of the chimney from slow disintegration from rainwater, it breaks up sparks coming from the chimney, and most importantly it prevents animals from nesting or otherwise exploring your chimney. Call a chimney sweep, mason, or roofer to order one. If it's difficult to look up (or down!) your chimney to be sure it's clear, a mirror and a flashlight will usually solve that problem.

Creosote buildup in chimneys is the principal reason for dangerous chimney fires. To reduce the amount of creosote collecting inside the chimney, burn hardwood (broadleaf flowering trees—such as oak, maple, and fruit trees) rather than softwood (conifers—such as pine, spruce, hemlock, and fir).

Floors

The maintenance requirements for several types of floors are discussed below. What's most important for all types of floors, however, is to minimize the amount of dirt ground into them. So vacuum, vacuum, vacuum. If you do this as often as is necessary to keep grit and grime from being caught between shoes and the floor, your floors will look great for years. Damp-mop or dust-mop between vacuuming sessions. No type of interior floor should be sloshed with water when cleaning. With this in mind, Amy Conway, who has written a number of the "Homekeeping" articles in *Martha Stewart Living,* offers this sound advice: "The best thing you can do for your floors is to kick off your shoes at the end of the day." I couldn't agree more.

Cement. Seal garage cement floors with a transparent concrete seal or an all-purpose seal from a paint store. The manufacturer's directions mainly involve getting the floor very clean before applying the sealer. *Do not* paint garage floors because oil and grease (and sometimes car tires) aren't compatible with paint. You can seal or paint basement floors, but don't paint these either if moisture is a problem.

Ceramic Tile. Please see the separate **Ceramic Tile** section, page 46.

Marble and Slate. Please see the separate **Stone Building Materials** section.

Quarry Tile. This very porous tile should be sealed with a product designed for it. The finish sealer you choose will affect how the tile looks, so if you want a natural-looking low sheen, don't apply a finish that will produce a glasslike shine.

Terrazzo. A penetrating sealer should be applied to new terrazzo floors to retard stain absorption. Resealing may be needed occasionally. Buffing helps restore the natural sheen of the stone.

Wood. Varnish as a floor finish has virtually disappeared, and along with it the high-maintenance, on-your-hands-and-knees paste wax that I still have nightmares about. Now most wood floors have a hard, plastic-like finish usually referred to as polyurethane, urethane, or Varathane. It requires much less maintenance because it is a no-wax finish.

The admonition to "vacuum, vacuum, vacuum" still applies to these floors. In addition, the most important maintenance advice are two *not*'s: Do *not* apply wax or a coat of acrylic floor finish. Do *not* wash the floor with any soap-based or even many detergent floor cleaners. They can leave a film that will prevent proper adhesion when it's time to apply another coat or two of polyurethane. Wash *only* with a dilute ammonia solution ($^{1}/_{2}$ to $^{3}/_{4}$ cup clear ammonia to 1 gallon water) or a neutral cleaner formulated for these floors.

Food Processors

Besides normal cleaning, to keep yours running well and to avoid bending the blades, add food in small amounts, and don't process items like ice, grains, dried fruits, and coffee beans. If the blades get bent or pitted, replace the blade assembly rather than trying to bend them back into shape or polish them.

Freezers

Freezers work most efficiently in a cool, dry location. The ambient room temperature shouldn't go much below 40°F for manual-defrost freezers and much below 60°F for frost-free freezers. Don't crowd things around the freezer: leave some room on both sides, the top, and the back for air exchange. Adjust the leveling as needed. An upright freezer should be tilted very slightly back so the door swings shut on its own when released.

For manual-defrost models, defrosting should be done annually, or when the frost is between one-quarter- and one-half-inch thick. Turn the freezer off, and unload the food into cooler chests or into boxes lined with plenty of newspapers or blankets. (Or do it when it's freezing outside—and just set the food on the deck. Somebody should keep an eye on the dog, however.)

If your freezer has a defrost drain, remove the drain plug from inside and place a shallow pan underneath. Have a second shallow pan handy, or place a bucket nearby for easier emptying. Lacking a defrost drain, use a large sponge or turkey baster. Place a bucket nearby to wring or empty into. A few towels to catch drips are a good idea. Put pans of hot water in the freezer with the door open, and direct air from a fan (placed outside the freezer) into the freezer to speed defrosting. Reheat the water when it cools off. Use a plastic spatula or scraper to remove frost when it starts to melt.

If you own a wet/dry shop vacuum, there is an easier, faster way to defrost. Melt the ice by blowing air into the freezer, then use it to suck up the water. Once the frost is removed, clean well with Red Juice and a cleaning cloth. Inspect and clean the door gasket. You might as well wash the outside at the same time. **Note:** Manufacturers recommend emptying and cleaning even frost-free models on an annual basis.

Move the freezer, if needed, to brush or vacuum the condenser coils. Frequency of cleaning depends on location, dirt, number of animals in the

household, and so forth. In general, it should be done often enough to keep the coils reasonably free of dust and hair (see **Refrigerators**).

In the event of a power failure, *don't* open the freezer for any reason except to stave off starvation. The food will stay frozen correspondingly longer if you don't open it "just to check." Especially with an upright freezer, when you open the door the cold air literally falls out, and the contents will warm up quite quickly from that point forward. Adding dry ice at the rate of two pounds per cubic foot of freezer space will keep foods frozen for up to four days, according to a recent Whirlpool owner's manual. Speaking of such cheery events, a freezer alarm that will alert you to a power failure is a good idea, especially if you have a freezer full of New York strip steaks and Alaskan king crab legs. If at all possible, put the freezer on its own electrical circuit, and, of course, don't select a receptacle that can be turned off with a switch or pull chain.

Furniture

Position furniture so there is enough room between it and the wall (or anything else) for the vacuum head to fit. If you don't leave this space, the furniture has to be moved or the vacuum disassembled just about every time you clean.

The scratches and gouges furniture legs inflict upon floors of all types are abundant, ugly, and expensive (if not impossible) to repair. Yet there is a cheap and easy solution—surface protectors. Even though the legs of most furniture have a metal, plastic, or rubber protector preinstalled at their base, it is there to protect the leg and not necessarily the surface below. However, there is practically no furniture with legs, almost none with wheels, and even some with neither (for example, speakers) that doesn't need a surface protector installed to protect the floor below.

Surface protectors of all types are available at hardware and other stores. For furniture legs on hard floors (wood, vinyl, tile, stone) I prefer carpet-like protectors that can be permanently attached to the legs so they don't have to be repositioned whenever the furniture is moved. For furniture legs with wheels, a coaster is called for. Furniture on carpeting also requires a coaster, with or without spikes to keep the carpet from being crushed. Cork pads work well on stereo speakers as they also help improve the sound, in addition to protecting the surface they're sitting on. **Note:**

Even with protectors in place, especially with carpet or felt protectors that can trap grit and grime, don't slide heavy furniture if you can lift it instead.

The following are additional maintenance subjects for specific types of furniture.

Fabric. Apply a stain-resistant product such as Scotchgard. If it's an option when you purchase the furniture, take it.

Leather. Manufacturers have widely different opinions about how to maintain leather. I suppose this is due to the widely varying qualities and finishes available, but here are some steps that are generally agreed upon:

1. As with fabric furniture, if you're offered a pretreatment option when purchasing leather furniture, take it! This treatment contains protectors against staining and soiling. It also helps keep the leather soft and supple. Some of them (such as Guardsman, when applied professionally) offer a warranty that covers stains, cracking, and even cuts, rips, and burns. Be sure to ask if and when the piece needs to be retreated.
2. Don't position leather furniture in direct sunlight or very close to a heating vent or fireplace. This is especially important for aniline-dyed or unfinished leathers. Their light color fades quickly.

3. Dust or carefully vacuum when you do your regular weekly or bi-weekly housecleaning. Dust and dirt are just as abrasive and damaging to leather as they are to the other surfaces in a house. In fact, dirt may be even more damaging to leather because it migrates to and concentrates at seams. These seams are bound together with thread, and if the grit isn't removed regularly, it can cut right though them—something that happens with auto seats with distressing regularity.

4. Once every year or two, clean with a leather cleaner. Or alternate between cleaning the entire piece and cleaning just those areas exposed to sweat and oily hair. There are at least two types of leather cleaners: surface cleaners and soap cleaners. Find which works best for your furniture by testing both. You're also testing for colorfastness, so conduct the test in that world-famous inconspicuous place. Allow the leather to dry completely after the first test before starting the second test.

Product instructions should include whether to use a sponge or soft cloth. You should dab or gently wipe, but not rub, the surface. Don't forget to slip a sheet of plastic under the furniture before starting this project. Don't let moisture get underneath the legs of the furniture, where rust can develop and stain the carpet. Tip the leather chair or couch forward (sup-

ported by its arms or by a coffee table or ottoman) so you can work on the back. This also creates a convenient place to put the cushions to clean. Do them first, starting with the edges and then the top and bottom. Set them on wax paper (or plastic wrap or a garbage bag), lean them against a wall similarly protected, and let them dry. Clean the back and tilt the furniture into its upright position. Stand behind it to clean the top of the back cushions. Then clean the rest of it except the lower front panel. Finally, tip the furniture onto its back and clean the front panel without having to get on your hands and knees. **Note:** Leather is much more vulnerable to stretching and other damage when it's wet or damp.

Follow up the cleaning by reconditioning with an agent to restore oil and nourishment to the leather. This will remoisturize leather, keep it soft and pliable, and make it more resistant to cracking and scuffing. Some say to use one that contains wax, which protects leather in the same way that it protects paint on a car. Again, pretest to be sure you like the feel on your furniture.

Whether the leather is color-coated (what most of us have) or has a dyed "unfinished" look (usually called aniline or semi-aniline) makes a big difference when there is a spill or other accident. Color-coated leathers are quite resistant to stains. Aniline and semi-aniline finishes are next, and suede and other rough unfinished leathers are practically nonmaintainable. Unfinished leather readily absorbs liquids (like red Kool-Aid) and greasy, oily stuff (from Grandfather's hair when he falls asleep after Thanksgiving dinner, for example). The good news about oily spots is they're often so completely absorbed into most types of leather that they eventually disappear. Because of the surface and nature of unfinished leather, even leather creams can cause blotches. Wipe unfinished leather with a damp cloth or an untreated dust cloth regularly, and protect it from accidents with particular care.

Call in a professional if the leather has a serious stain such as ink or red wine—especially on unfinished leather. But here are the steps to take if you want to spot-clean the furniture. (Pretest any procedure once.) Some dirt can be removed with an art gum eraser, but be careful—you don't want to make a clean spot that will be more visible than the dirt was.

Greasy Stains: Wipe off any surplus stain as quickly as possible with a cleaning cloth or paper towel. This is the type of spot that should eventually disappear into the leather. If you wish to hurry up the process, use soap and water (Ivory would work). Dampen the area and dab gently, then rinse with clean water and stop. Don't soak through the leather. Absorb liquid with a cleaning cloth, allow to air-dry, and then polish the surface with a dry soft cloth.

Water-Soluble Stains: Dab with a sponge saturated in clean warm water. Dab an area larger than the stain, and absorb the water with a clean dry cloth. As with a stain on the carpet or other furniture, work inward toward the center of the stain. Place the piece of furniture off-limits until it has completely dried. Don't hasten the drying process with heat. After it's dry, polish the area gently with a soft dry cloth.

Wicker. Dust regularly with a dusting brush, or vacuum with the brush attachment. Spills can soak into the wicker and stain permanently, so remove them promptly. Rain, direct sunlight, and dew are all damaging. Indoor heat dries wicker and makes it crackle and creak when sat upon. An occasional wiping with a damp sponge may help, but it's probably too late once it gets that dry. Better maintenance involves placing it away from direct heat and sun and maintaining an adequate level of humidity in your home.

As startling as the idea may seem, raw wicker (other than bamboo) should be literally washed every two years. Either move the item outside or put it in the shower, and then gently scrub with a soft brush and a bucket of warm water and dishwashing detergent. Rinse with a garden hose or the shower nozzle. It's important to dry the chair quickly, so put it in the sun, and/or use a hair dryer or fan. Don't use the chair for several days while it continues to dry. Then check for new sharp or fuzzy places caused by the washing. Remove them with fine sandpaper and put the chair back in service. **Note:** This procedure is for raw wicker. Painted wicker may start to peel if washed. Some wicker has wooden parts. If so, don't wet these either. Wash both with a sponge dampened in sudsy water. Then wipe with a sponge dipped in clean water and allow to dry thoroughly.

Glass. Although glass used for tabletops is heavy and strong, it can all too easily be scratched—especially by jewelry, utensils, or even other glass. This fact, and their perpetual need for cleaning, is a big drawback to glass tabletops. They are beautiful when new, but they will get scratched soon after they're exposed to life outside a showroom (besides showing dust and fingerprints vastly more than any other type of tabletop). A standard coffee mug can wreak havoc on a glass tabletop if it's carelessly moved across its surface. Moving most other hard items across the glass will also scratch without fail. Use coasters, place mats, hot pads, or even newspapers if that's all that's handy to protect glass from these subtle and nearly constant assaults. Don't place a lamp, candlestick, picture frame, or other item on a glass surface without first putting surface protectors on its bottom. The same self-adhesive felt or flannel protectors used on picture frames will work just fine.

Wood. It's the finish of the wood that determines what sort of maintenance must be performed. Be sure to ask about the finish when you purchase furniture.

As mentioned, different finishes require certain products to maintain them. Once you've started with one type of product, don't switch unless you have a compelling reason. For example, if you apply oil to a finish that has polish on it, you will end up with a gooey mess that's difficult to get rid of. Clean the surface thoroughly or, better yet, remove the finish entirely before changing furniture care products.

Oil finishes will benefit from an additional coat of oil rubbed in once a year or so. Polyurethane's plastic-like finishes are much more resistant than traditional varnish to moisture, spills, heat, and the other dangers lurking in our households. Accordingly, they don't need a protective coat of furniture polish or wax. Just dust, and wipe occasionally with Red Juice as needed to remove fingerprints and so forth. Varnish and shellac are perked up by an occasional application of furniture polish, but no more than a couple of times a year. (An exception would be furniture that gets very heavy use, such as a varnish-coated dining room table that should be cleaned and polished after each use.)

Garbage Disposers

It's unwise to throw everything in the kitchen into the garbage disposer just because it's there. Save fibrous things such as artichoke leaves, corn husks, carrots, and banana peels, plus grease, clam/oyster shells, and bones for the garbage, and, of course, plastic, porcelain, and any type of metal. The disposer drain will clog just as easily as other drains, but don't use drain cleaners in the disposer's drain. And don't leave food in the disposer for hours on end. Seemingly benign tea leaves or coffee grounds have enough acidity to eventually corrode the blades or housing itself.

Not using enough water or not running the water long enough after grinding are two main causes of clogs in the disposer's drainage piping. Turn the cold water on before you turn on the disposer. Continue running water until all the material is ground and the disposer is running freely. The people at In-Sink-Erator—who know more about ground-up crud than the rest of us care to imagine—recommend keeping the cold water on (at full blast) for fifteen seconds after grinding is finished, but with the disposer still operating. Keep the water running a few moments longer after turning off the disposer. These steps are especially important if you happen to be grinding up some stale rice or pasta that can swell after being waterlogged. (One of our customers ground up a half a bag of rice in a disposer and then immediately turned off the disposer and the water. The next day he returned to find a solid mass of swollen rice paste from the sink to the main waste line. It was not a fun morning.)

Avoiding clogs is quite easy if you follow the above guidelines. If your disposer has a problem, however, here's what to do. If you know that the jam was caused by a solid object like a spoon, shut the power off and remove the object with tongs.

If the spoon is impossible to remove or if it's jammed because of fibrous material or another hard object, you'll have to work the flywheel free by moving it back and forth with the power still off. This is easy enough to do with disposers that came with a six-sided wrench inserted in the bottom of the unit. If yours didn't come with this handy-dandy wrench, next best bet is a specialized tool (available for $8 or so at hardware stores) that has a handle on top and a lever of sorts on the business end. The last choice is your own pry-bar of some kind. The most popular choice—based on availability and proximity—is a broom handle. In either case, the idea is to rotate the flywheel backward, thereby freeing it along with whatever had jammed it. This seems easy enough to do in theory, but the trick is to figure out backward from forward. First go find a nice, strong flashlight. Aim it so you can see what's going on down there—like what direction the thing was going in when it jammed. A helper would be nice—if for no other reason than to give a second opinion about the state of affairs, which, of course, will be the exact opposite of yours.

The broom handle is a somewhat dangerous lever because of its length. It's quite easy to loosen plumbing connections or even the whole unit if you apply too much leverage with a broom handle (or any of these tools, in fact). Just don't be too stubborn about your interpretation of backward and forward. If your prying isn't loosening the jam, try the other direction—preferably before your efforts succeed in loosening the plumbing.

One of these methods should release whatever it was that caused the jam, and it can now be lifted out with tongs. It really isn't smart to reach into a disposer—even if the power is off—although I have to admit that I do it myself. If there are toddlers around who might turn on the switch, unplug the unit or tape the switch in the off position.

If the disposer still won't start after you've cleared the clog, the motor may be overheated. Wait fifteen minutes, make sure the power switch is off, and then press the reset button. (Most disposers have a red reset button on the underside of the unit.) No luck? Check the circuit breaker or fuse. Still no luck? Call the plumber.

Having been warned about what *not* to put into the disposer, you may be surprised to read that experts recommend grinding up certain hard materials to scour out the inside of the unit. Al Hale, who has been in the appliance business in San Francisco for more than forty years, recommends grinding up a few handfuls of ice cubes once a month. This will scour the disposer clean and help keep it smelling fresh. Grind ice the same way you would grind anything else. Lest you think Al is a bit odd, one reputable manufacturer (In-Sink-Erator) recommends grinding up small bones and fruit pits for the same reason.

Specialized products are available for cleaning the inside of the disposer. Disagreeable odors are the tip-off that this needs to be done. However, it shouldn't be a problem if you use the disposer properly and grind ice occasionally. You can also clean it yourself as follows: Turn it off, tape the switch in the off position, and/or unplug the unit. Use a scouring pad (I suggest a white pad impregnated with dish soap) and reach down to clean the underside of the rubber baffle and as much of the interior of the disposer as possible. Then put a stopper in the disposer opening and add water to the sink, along with a generous dose of baking soda. Mix this solution with your hand or a wooden spoon and unplug the disposer. Let the solution wash away the loosened food, grease, and so on, but don't turn on the disposer until you need it again. In the meantime, the remaining baking soda will continue to deodorize the interior.

If you have a septic tank, use the garbage disposer about as often as you have your appendix removed. Not many home septic systems were designed for the volume of waste that a disposer adds. If you run much food through it, you incur the very real risk that the entire septic system could become plugged up and quit working prematurely (see **Septic Systems**).

Granite See **Stone Building Materials.**

Grout

Most grout is made of sand and cement, so it's rough and porous. And the pores are easily filled with soap scum, dirt, coffee, or any number of other household stain-makers. Maintain grout by filling the pores with an appropriate sealer *first* (check at a good hardware, paint, or home-supply store). Sealing makes the grout easier to clean and reduces permanent stains from dirt or mildew—whether you use an acidic cleaner or not (see **Note,** page 106). Reseal once or twice a year.

The alkaline cement in grout, like marble and some other natural products, is attacked by acidic cleaners. An acidic cleaner (e.g., Tile Juice and others) can slowly erode the cement from the grout and eventually make the surface rougher and therefore harder to clean. It may also affect colored grout by making it lighter or mottled. **Note:** Because my house has very hard water, because acidic cleaners work best on hard-water stains, and because the damage it causes to sealed grout is minimal and gradual, I continue to use a mild acidic cleaner (Tile Juice), but I'm careful to rinse thoroughly when finished.

Hair Dryers

Hair dryers have an air intake that eventually becomes clogged with hair and lint, which is why they often smell like burning hair. In fact, most small appliances with a fan quickly become incredibly dusty and dirty. If it becomes clogged, the hair dryer motor can burn up in short order. You can usually keep it clean without disassembly by using a toothbrush and vacuum cleaner. If you do disassemble it (usually requiring only a screwdriver), clean the fan blades and remove hair wrapped around the base of the fan or tangled around the heating coil. Clean dried hair spray with alcohol and cotton swabs or paper towels. To reassemble, first make sure the cord is properly seated, then start all screws, then go back and tighten them.

Heaters, Electric

If the cord of any type of electric heater gets hot, take the heater in for servicing.

Baseboard Electric Heaters. Once installed, there's not much to be done to keep a baseboard heater working properly. It's a good idea, especially if you have pets, to vacuum or brush the heating elements thoroughly at the start of each heating season. Dust, pet hair, spiders, cobwebs, and the like that collect inside will be cooked until they're sizzled, but during the process it will be rather stinky.

Portable Electric Fan Heaters. These can be convective or ceramic, but in either case they have to pull air in through vents to operate properly. These vents must be kept open or the unit will overheat. If the heater has a filter, remove it when it's dirty, wash it with dish soap and water, and allow it to dry thoroughly before replacing it. Remove dust from the fan and grilles with the brush attachment of a vacuum. Accumulated lint and debris can ignite, so remove interior dust with the vacuum's crevice attachment. Before storing the heater for the summer, protect the cord from accidents by wrapping it up neatly. I prefer to store things that are used only part of the year in a box or a garbage bag—clearly labeled, of course—so they won't gather dust while they're out of service.

Radiator Oil Heaters. They're easy. No significant maintenance. Just clean with a vacuum or wipe with Red Juice and a cleaning cloth when doing your routine housecleaning.

Heating and Cooling Systems

Household heating, ventilation, and air-conditioning (HVAC) systems include the furnace and air conditioner, ducts, return-air vents, room vents, and filters. Newer home construction often includes a single unit that both heats and cools. Whether your system is gas, electric, or oil, the following general maintenance steps apply. Hot-water heating systems and steam-heating systems have different maintenance steps and are not discussed here.

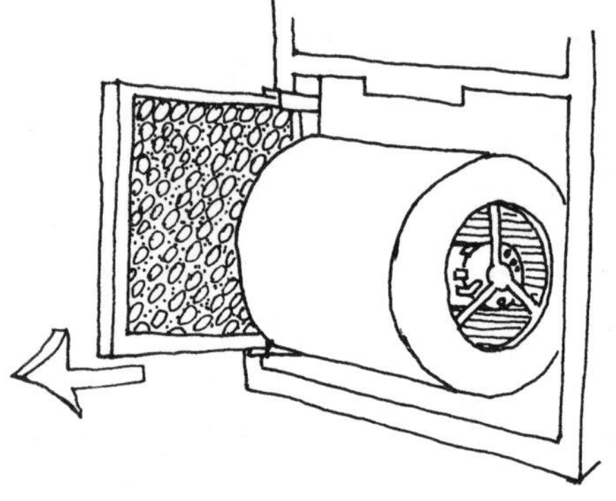

Furnace. Change or clean the filter monthly during the heating season. Keep a supply on hand so you don't have the excuse that you don't have time to run to the hardware store to get one. Change the filter even if it doesn't look very dirty. By the time a filter is really visibly dirty, you've waited too long. At that point, air circulation is decreased, and the amount of dust put back into circulation has increased. In fact, if your house is particularly dusty and/or you have pets, filters should be changed even more often.

Vacuum the blower (usually behind a filter) yearly or every six months if needed. This can be an easy or a difficult chore depending on the type of furnace, its age, and its design. There are often one or more spots on motors (especially on older furnaces) that need a few drops of oil once or twice a year. Have your furnace serviced by a professional before the cold season yearly or every other year. **Note:** If you would like to perform annual maintenance on the furnace and perhaps other major appliances yourself, the advice from here is, don't try to learn how from the owner's manual. It's apt not to be of much help. Instead, hire a professional to do the service, then observe, ask questions, and take notes.

At least for any that you can access, check ducts for loose connections and repair with duct tape. It's surprising that they come loose, but the force of the air and its drying effect create leaks and make duct tape separate over time. Not only do leaks waste hot (or

cooled) air, they allow pests of all sizes to take up residence. I've had mice as well as a full litter of kittens find their way into the ducts of my home. Much, much smaller things accumulate in ducts even if there are no leaks. Mildew, mold, dust mites, and bacteria are examples. Cleaning inside the ducts is not a part of the annual or biannual servicing of a unit, but they should be cleaned by a professional every seven to ten years. If you suffer allergies or asthma, you may have to have them cleaned more often to remove allergens.

If the system has a standing pilot light, keep it burning all year. It will help keep the furnace dry and help prevent corrosion, and the furnace will be ready to use during any unexpected cold snap.

An **electronic air filter** can be added to most modern HVAC systems. It does a great job of removing pollutants to make indoor air healthier. It also greatly reduces the amount of dust (and, it logically follows, the amount of time spent dusting) in a home. Its metal filters are washable and also require monthly cleaning during the heating (and cooling, if appropriate) months. With the power off, remove and wash the filter with soap and water—or put it into the dishwasher. Rinse, and allow to dry completely before reinstalling. These filters aren't expensive, so replace them whenever they get damaged. Once a year, slide out the electronic cells and carefully wash them in the same way. **Note:** As with all filters, no matter how efficient they are at removing particulate from the air that passes through, they stay efficient only if they remain clean. An electronic air filter may be rated at 90 percent to 95 percent overall efficiency, but the rating applies only when it has a clean filter cell! Efficiency ratings fall off dramatically when the filter is not kept clean.

Another unit that can be added to existing HVAC systems is a humidifier. According to Janice Papolos in *The Virgin Homeowner,* central humidifiers must be cleaned weekly during the heating season, or they can become a breeding ground for mold spores and germs. She suggests sticking to a room humidifier if your schedule doesn't allow for this maintenance. A room humidifier also needs weekly cleaning, but at least it is more accessible (see **Humidifiers**).

Central Air Conditioners. As with a window air conditioner, your central air-conditioning unit should not be installed in the direct sun. Don't let vegetation around it obstruct its air intake.

Have a professional look at it every one to three years, depending on usage and age. Here are a few guidelines: If you use it twenty-four hours a day for extended periods of time, or if it's also a combination furnace/air conditioner that operates throughout the winter, have the unit serviced once a year. If you use it only during the day and it is fairly new, you might have it serviced every third year. The average life span is fifteen years. After ten years or so, have it serviced annually regardless of use.

Double-check with the service person about how to reach the parts to be cleaned and about any other routine maintenance (such as oiling the motor) that should be performed before he or she returns.

Here's what you should do if you don't have the unit serviced, or in the years that it isn't serviced. Prune back plant growth that could impede airflow to and from the unit, but leave growth that will help shade it. Use a brush and/or hose to clean the outside condensing unit. This involves removing a panel and/or the fan grill. Use a high-pressure nozzle and water to remove leaves, dirt, and so forth. Squirt water from inside out and from outside in. Remove debris from the inside floor of the unit. If needed, use a fin comb (available from appliance stores) to straighten condenser coil fins. Wipe fan blades clean.

The second part of the air-conditioning unit contains

the evaporator (cooling) coils. They're usually located inside the house at the top or bottom of the furnace (although if your furnace and air conditioner are a single unit, they could be on the furnace side of the outdoor unit). The drain pan should be cleaned once a year and the plastic drainpipe checked to be sure it isn't clogged. It's normal for water to drip from this pipe, so it's important that it isn't clogged and that the water flows to an appropriate drain. (If the evaporator unit is outside, also check to be sure that wasps or other critters haven't taken up residence in the pipe during periods of non-use.) It's also possible for this pipe to be plugged with algae. If it's plugged, remove the pipe by removing the tape holding it in place or by sawing through it. Clean the pipe with a hose and either spray it thoroughly with 50 percent bleach solution or soak it in that solution for a few minutes. Rinse, and reinstall the pipe with tape.

Also inside the house, vacuum discharge registers as often as needed to keep them free of dust and lint. Remove them once a year to clean the back. Vacuum inside the duct as far as the vacuum wand will reach.

Check, and be prepared to clean or replace, air filters monthly during the hot season (see Rule 9). Needless to say, this will be easier to do—not to mention more likely to happen at all—if you keep spare filters handy. Don't run the unit without a filter in place, and allow any filter you just washed to dry completely before reinstalling it.

If your system has an electronic air filter, it must be cleaned as described under **Furnace,** page 108.

If you don't use the air conditioner for months on end, turn it on once a month during the off-season to keep the condenser happy. It has a tendency to stick after long periods of inactivity. Sticking in this case means the air conditioner won't start in the spring when you need it, and a repair visit will be required.

Window Air Conditioners. If you install a window air conditioner in a cool and shady spot instead of one that's in the hot afternoon sun, it will run less, cool better, cost less to operate, and last longer.

No matter where it's installed, make sure the mounting is well sealed. Air leaks are an expensive waste of energy, and they are an entry point for rainwater, which will damage the wall. Foam stripping and/or caulk was usually applied when the air conditioner was first installed. If you're doing the installing, put one inch of foam rubber or some similar material under and over the unit. This will also reduce noise. Check all four sides annually, and repair or replace foam rubber or other weather-stripping material as necessary.

Remove the unit in the winter, or make the installation more permanent by replacing the original fair-weather plastic side-panels with plywood. Then caulk around it and paint it.

Starting up the motor of an air conditioner puts a heavy demand on the electric circuitry. Window air conditioners generally aren't on their own ("dedicated") circuit, but it's a good idea if possible. Otherwise, be careful what shares the circuit with the unit, and don't plug anything into the other half of the same wall outlet. Also, keep the doors closed in the room to be cooled. Turning on ceiling fans will stir up the air and make it at least seem cooler. Window air conditioners can't cool the entire house. If you try, the result is apt to be a house that isn't comfortably cool, a higher electric bill, and an air conditioner that wears out before its time.

According to Franklynn Peterson's *How to Fix Damn Near Everything*, air-conditioner problems can arise from too many people adjusting the thermostat too often. Once you have set the thermostat where you want it, pull the knob off and hide it if necessary. When you're home and it's hot, you can change it as needed. This seems a bit severe, but it's a maintenance option.

Don't obstruct the flow in or out of the front of the air conditioner. Curtains, houseplants, and furniture should be two feet or more away from the front grill. Keep outdoor obstructions two feet away also. Running the unit when the temperature is below 60°F outside can also block airflow by frosting the coils.

If certain parts of an air conditioner gets dirty, it may not provide cool air. Here is a list of annual maintenance tasks to keep it running well. Re-

member to unplug the unit before performing maintenance.

1. Clean the front grill. It's best to have someone work with you because to do this, you may have to slide the machine out. (You may also have to refer to the owner's manual to find out how to remove the front grill. There are usually screws or release clips, but they may be hidden from view.) Slide the unit out of the window far enough so you can get at the parts that need maintenance. Move a table into place to support the air conditioner during this time. Wash the front panel with Red Juice, a toothbrush, and cleaning cloths. There are plenty of little grills and louvers, so the toothbrush comes in quite handy. This is the part that's usually so dusty and dirty that it makes a one-year-old unit look like it's fifteen years old, so take the time to clean it well.

2. Clean the coils and fins. You must remove the wraparound housing to do this, but it usually takes just a screwdriver or a socket wrench to do so. If the screws are difficult to remove, apply a few drops of penetrating oil. Use a brush, the vacuum with a brush attachment, and/or Red Juice and a cleaning cloth to clean the condenser coils and fins (at the rear of the unit) and the evaporator coils and fins (toward the front of the unit). Bent fins should be straightened with a fin comb, which is available at appliance parts stores. Wipe the fan blades and straighten any bends.

3. Check the rubber or plastic drain tube and/or drain hole at the same time. If either is clogged, flush a 50 percent bleach solution through the tube with a turkey baster. (Wear old clothes.) Position a bucket to catch the solution. After a few minutes, flush water through the same tube to purge the bleach. If flushing doesn't work, insert a wire into the tube and dislodge whatever might be there. If the unit has a drain pan where water collects, also flush it with the bleach solution to kill algae and inhibit their regrowth, and once again finish by flushing with water.

Running an air conditioner condenses water, which can give rise to unpleasant odors. If the air conditioner starts to stink halfway through the season, you may have to reclean the areas just described. In other words, once again unclog the drain hole and the drain tube. A toothbrush or thin bottle brush may come in handy. Then pour in a cup or so of the same bleach and water solution, and then rinse the drain pan.

4. Inspect for rust during the cleaning operation. Remove rust with steel wool and touch up bare metal with rust-resistant metal primer. Some air conditioners need lubrication for the blower motor. If yours does, and you don't provide it, the motor will get progressively noisier and start to have other problems within a few seasons. Check the owner's manual for what to lubricate, and then either do it or have a professional service it every year or two.

Change or clean the filter behind the front grill once a month during the season it's in use. Clean metal mesh or foam filters by washing in hot soapy water, rinsing, and drying. Replace disposable filters.

Heat Pump. Clean the coils once a year. Turn the power off and remove the top and side panels to access the coils. Use a garden hose with a high-pressure nozzle to remove leaves, dirt, and debris. Aim the nozzle from the inside pointing out and from the outside pointing in. Use your fingers or tweezers to remove leaves and so forth that resist the water and remain stuck in the coil fins. Don't use a screwdriver or other tool that could damage the fins. For the same reason, use a fin comb to straighten coil fins rather than a screwdriver.

Hinges See **Doors and Door Hardware.**

Hot Plates

If the plug is detachable from the base, plug it into the hot plate first, and then into the electric outlet. Spilled foods can cause shorts or other electrical problems, so don't overfill cooking containers, and wipe up spills ASAP. Use Red Juice and a cleaning cloth, along with a toothbrush and a white pad, if necessary.

Humidifiers

Without careful maintenance, some humidifiers can spew mold, fungi, and dust into the air that you and your family breathe. Therefore it's particularly important to replace filters and clean the tank with a bleach solution according to the instructions in the owner's manual. Some humidifiers have hard-to-clean foam belts and drums that also need cleaning in a bleach or other antibacterial solution. Some have evaporator pads or belts, water trays, and other parts where hard-water deposits accumulate. Remove these by soaking in a 50 percent white vinegar and water solution overnight. You can go all the way to 100 percent vinegar to speed up the process.

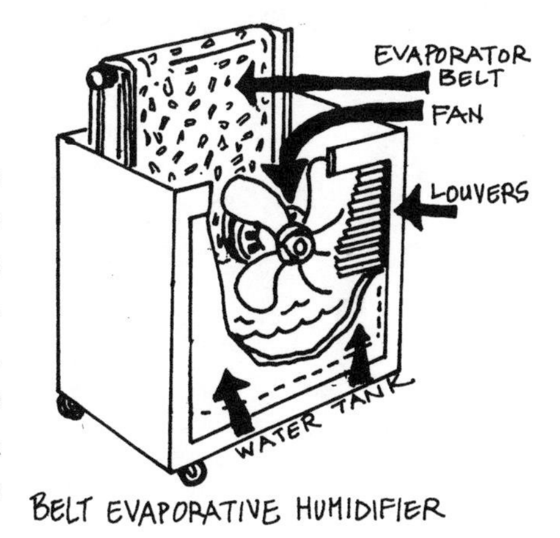

BELT EVAPORATIVE HUMIDIFIER

Inspect the pad and other parts of the humidifier weekly until you know how often different parts need sterilizing (the bleach solution) or cleaning (the vinegar solution). Replace evaporator pads when they are no longer soft and spongy. Using distilled water will greatly reduce maintenance problems due to mineral buildup.

Don't place wood furniture or anything electronic too close to humidifiers. Also keep audio- and videotapes, computer discs, and paper well away from them, as humidifiers can promote the growth of black mildew.

Irons

It's best to empty a steam iron while it's hot so heat will dry out the water reservoir. Store it upright. This will help prevent rust and pitting of the sole plate, but it doesn't help with hard-water problems.

Most problems with irons come from hard-water (mineral) deposits left inside the appliance. If your iron has a self-cleaning feature to remove hard-water buildup, use it with every ironing job. If not, when your iron starts to show signs of buildup—by spraying erratically, for example—it will probably benefit from the same treatment used to rid coffeemakers of hard water. Pour a cup of 50 percent water and 50 percent white vinegar solution into your iron, and run the entire amount through the steam mechanism—but not while ironing clothes, of course! Instead, place the iron bottom on a metal rack over a broiling pan. Then rinse by refilling with plain water and run that through the same way—again before ironing any clothes. Mineral deposits that are visible in the steam vents in the bottom of the iron can often be forced out using a strong wire.

Some manufacturers recommend distilled water for irons; others recommend plain tap water. It depends on how your particular model generates steam. If you have hard water in your neck of the woods, using distilled water will help avoid the hard-water buildup that clogs nozzle holes and causes the steam mechanism to work improperly. **Note:** Water processed through a water softener isn't a substitute for distilled water. The water softener adds salts to the water that could harm the iron as well as your clothes.

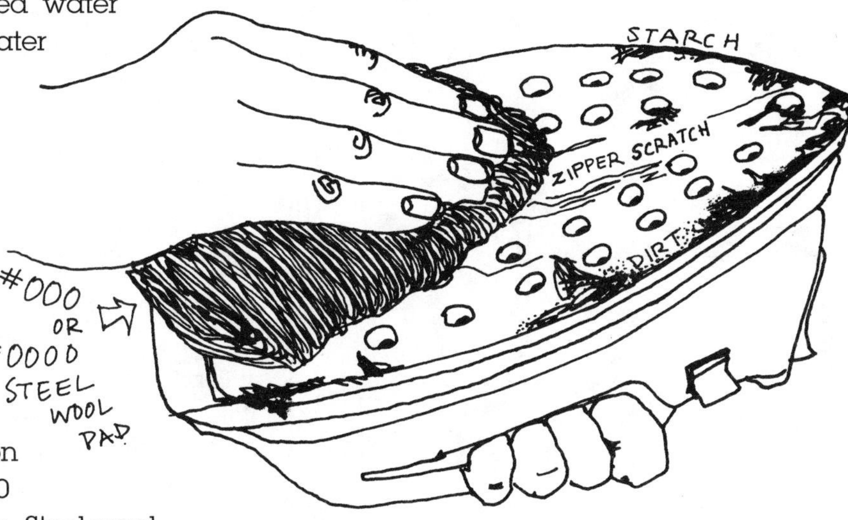

If the metal sole of an iron gets encrusted with burned-on starch or dirt, clean it off with #000 or #0000 steel wool and Red Juice. Steel wool will also remove small scratches. Avoid creating scratches in the first place by not ironing over buttons or zippers.

Lampshades

I've noticed that lampshades are one of the things that seem to be invisible to some housecleaners—the same way miniblinds and houseplants often are. For fabric lampshades, use a dusting brush and/or a vacuum with a brush attachment, and dust them as you do your regular cleaning. Hard-surface lampshades—parchment, plastic-coated, fiberglass, mica, and so on—can be vacuumed in the same way or can be feather-dusted instead. They should also be wiped a few times a year with a cleaning cloth sprayed lightly with Red Juice.

If it's been a number of years since anyone dusted a fabric lampshade, it should be washed—or tossed, if it's not worth the effort. Do one or the other, but don't continue to ignore it. Wash it by filling a sink or large bucket with enough warm water to cover the lampshade. Add some dish soap, swish around to mix well, and then dip the shade up and down in the water. Gently. (If parts are glued to the fabric, either sew them on before you start this process or reglue them afterward—the former being the better choice.) When the solution gets dirty, replace it and repeat. Rinse in several changes of water. Hang the shade up to drip-dry. You will feel amazingly virtuous afterward.

Leaks See **Faucets** and **Bathtubs.**

Light Fixtures

It seems that if you look at it from the right angle, nearly every glass part of every light fixture in the world has a dirty film on it. Remove it rather painlessly by washing it in the dishwasher every few months or so.

Mattresses

Mattresses (and pillows and fabric furniture and carpets) are places where dust mites are fond of congregating. As we discussed in *Talking Dirt,* dust mites aren't usually a problem unless a family member is allergic to them. Even so, you don't have to ignore them—and regular vacuumings of a mattress gets rid of a few zillion or so at a time. Use the furniture attachment and be thorough. Switch to the crevice attachment to deep-clean around buttons.

A good mattress cover keeps the mattress from being soiled and allows you to wash away a few trillion more mites. Get one that you can wash in hot water and that is easy to install and remove.

If a mattress does get dirty, wash it with upholstery shampoo, following package directions. As with other upholstery, the trick is to use soapsuds (not soap and water) to do the cleaning and thereby avoid getting the mattress too wet. Clean a small area with a medium-bristle brush, blot well with a cleaning cloth, and move to the next area. Naturally, you must wait for the mattress to dry completely before using it again. A fan blowing across the mattress speeds drying, as does warm dry air.

In these days of mergers and acquisitions and national and multinational companies, it's increasingly rare to see an independent business of any kind. But there's one near my office on Market Street in San Francisco: McRoskey Airflex Mattress Co. Old building, old people, and wonderful handmade mattresses (not just my opinion, either). Just thinking about the company makes me smile. They've been making quality mattresses since 1899, and I hope they're still at it in 2099. Tony Uruburu, who helped me select at least one of my three McRoskey mattresses, and the rest of the staff have definite opinions on how to care for a mattress. Here's what they say to do:

- Do not bend the mattress from side to side or in a V shape. A "horse-shoe" bend from head to foot is harmless (and is a great help in elevators and restricted entrances and when turning your mattress).

- After two weeks of initial use, flip the mattress over from head to foot.
- After another two weeks, spin the mattress around from head to foot (i.e., don't lift or flip it this time).
- Continue this sequence for a cycle of four turnings.
- After four weeks, reverse the box springs from end to end. (My suggestion: Vacuum it while it's exposed.)
- From here onward, occasional turnings are helpful.
- Vacuum or brush the surface and occasionally expose the surface to air.

Any questions about mattresses? Call Tony or anyone on the McRoskey staff (1-800-760-9600).

Microwave Ovens

As with a conventional oven, it's smarter to catch spatters right away than to let them land on all four sides of the oven's interior. When a loose cover will prevent splatters, use paper towels, plastic wrap, or wax paper. Put a paper towel or plate under food cooked directly on a shelf or the floor of the oven (e.g., a baked potato).

Microwave ovens seem to develop a unique B.O. Keep it to a minimum by opening the door to let it air out for a few minutes after cooking. Spray and wipe the inside with Red Juice and a cleaning cloth whenever you clean the kitchen. If odor continues to be a problem, an occasional wipe with baking soda and water does wonders.

Trying to microwave something too big could expose you to leaking microwave radiation or could damage the door or hinges. Check the gasket regularly to be sure it seals properly when closed. Meters that test for leaks are available for less than ten dollars.

Miniblinds

In my grumpy opinion, the ideal maintenance solution to the scourge of miniblinds is to avoid buying them in the first place. They're nearly impossible to maintain. Even if you win a complete houseful on *Wheel of Fortune,* opt for cash instead. (Just in case Mr. or Mrs. Levelor is reading this and is feeling a little bad [or mad], it's only the horizontal blinds that are so difficult to maintain. I think vertical ones are perfectly dandy.)

The first step in any effective maintenance program is to leave them in the fully "pulled up" position as often as possible. That is the only way to avoid the dust that otherwise collects, gathers moisture, and becomes more like a coat of adobe than a layer of dust.

The next maintenance necessity is regular dusting. Start within days of hanging them so you never get behind, because maintenance will not work if you ignore them until they have a visible, tenacious layer of dust. (Then they have to be washed, and that delightful chore is explained in *Talking Dirt.*) I prefer to dust them with the brush attachment of a vacuum cleaner. Other options are to use a feather duster or a dusting cloth. You need not dust every square inch of every slat each time you clean house, but dust some of them every time. For example, dust one or two rooms of blinds each time you do your regular housecleaning. Don't put this job off, telling yourself that you'll do them all in some marathon burst of cleaning fervor. There's too great a chance that such an energetic high may not arrive quite soon enough.

There are two other maintenance points of interest. One is that the blinds should be stabilized with one hand when dusting or handling so that they don't bang against the window frames. If they do, they will probably chip paint off the window frames and/or the slats themselves. Finally, don't bend a slat to peek through the blinds. Once a slat is bent, it's got a lifetime crease.

Mirrors

Here's what the National Association of Mirror Manufacturers has to say about caring for mirrors:

1. Don't use heavy-duty, harsh commercial "cleanup" solutions on mirrors. Most of them contain abrasives, alkalis, or acids—all of which are harmful to mirrors.
2. Do use any of these three types of recommended cleaners:
   A. Weak (5–10%) solutions of rubbing alcohol and water.
   B. Weak (5%) solutions of household ammonia and water.
   C. Weak (5%) solutions of white vinegar and water.
3. Don't use dirty or gritty rags, knives, scrapers, emery cloths, or other abrasive material for cleaning.
4. Do use a clean, soft rag or paper towel when cleaning mirrors.

5. Don't abuse the "critical edges" of the mirror. Most mirror failures are at the edges, where spillover solutions attack the backing at its most vulnerable point.
6. Do protect the edges and frame from spillover by applying the cleaner to the cloth rather than to the mirror. Also, it's a good practice to wipe exposed edges clean and dry after any cleaning.

The most important considerations are Numbers 5 and 6. Don't let cleaners, or even water, get into the crack between the frame and the mirror, where it will be wicked up and attack the backing of the mirror. We've all seen the result—misshapen dark stains spreading inward from the frame. One more thing: Blue Juice and any general glass cleaner in the known world are just fine for cleaning mirrors (except for plastic ones). It's not necessary to make your own cleaning potion from alcohol, ammonia, or vinegar.

Mixers, Hand-Held and Standing

To avoid serious damage to the rotating mixers, use a rubber spatula—not wood or metal—to scrape the bowl during use. Blocked air vents on the motor housing can cause the motor to overheat. Clean them with Red Juice and cotton swabs and/or vacuum with a brush attachment. The number one cause of mixer failure, according to California Electric Service in San Francisco, is overloading the mixer with too much dough.

Ovens

If it weren't for laziness—or thoughtlessness, I suppose—ovens wouldn't get dirty! Think about it. Ovens only get dirty from food that overflows its container and becomes baked onto the oven floor and walls. Change behavior (i.e., use large enough cooking containers), and the oven will stay clean. Aluminum foil won't solve the problem if the containers are still too small. Many ovens don't heat properly if foil is laid on the bottom or if the foil is too large or improperly placed. Foil on the racks themselves generally causes poor baking results. Even broilers shouldn't be lined with foil unless your oven manual gives the okay. (It's the same problem as with lining underneath stovetop burners. It concentrates the heat and can cause damage to the pan.) Use a large enough container or two smaller ones. Maintenance will be a snap because little is required.

As with other appliances with doors, check and keep clean the gasket around the oven door. If it's damaged, replace it. Don't clean the gasket of a self-cleaning oven. Just brush it with a toothbrush.

No matter how good the idea seems at the time, don't use an oven for temporary storage of things—most especially plastic things. The fateful day will come when you (forgetful) or someone else (unsuspecting) preheats the oven and . . .

Paintings

Situate a valuable painting on a wall that doesn't get direct sun or heat. Don't hang it over a heat register or a fireplace. Moderate temperatures and moderate humidity are best. Don't hang or store valuable paintings in or near a bathroom. Store them upright and let them lean forward when hung to limit the amount of dirt that settles and to allow air circulation.

Dust the painting and the frame with an ostrich-down feather duster each time you dust the rest of the house. Use a soft-bristle dusting brush or the brush attachment of a vacuum occasionally to remove dust from intricate frames. Don't vacuum the painting itself. Whether you should even dust the painting depends on the condition and/or value of the painting and the softness of the brush.

For paintings protected by glass, spray the cloth with Blue Juice and wipe the glass clean and dry. (But make sure it's really glass: Any glass

cleaner that contains alcohol shouldn't be used on Plexiglas. Use a specialized plastic cleaner.)

If the painting is yet to be covered, UV-resistant glass or Plexiglas is usually also a good idea.

To protect the walls from being scratched by the frame, install surface protectors on the back of at least the two lower corners, but all four corners is better. Self-adhesive flannel, plastic, cork, or velvet surface protectors—precut as dots or in sheets—are inexpensive and widely available in hardware and other stores.

If you have an extensive collection of art, the following is old news (goes along with your old money, perhaps), but if you're just starting to acquire a few art pieces, read on. Specific valuable items in a household—for example, the *Mona Lisa* or the crown jewels of England—are almost certainly not covered by your homeowner's insurance policy. A special rider to your policy may be required for you to be fully protected. At the very least, make a call to your insurance broker, and store receipts and photos of such items in a safe-deposit box.

Pets

Whether we pet lovers admit it or not, pets add a lot to home maintenance. And though size is a factor, the worst offenders can be quite small.

Oddly enough, The Clean Team's least favorite, most time-consuming pets to clean around are birds. As you perhaps suspected, big dogs are next. Here are a few strategies:

1. Train pets to enter through just one door. This door should be the one that's the most protected from weather, has the best mats, and is farthest from mud and related ilk. Leave a towel and/or brush there to use when the pet enters the house. If pets come to the wrong door, go to the correct one and call them to you. They will quickly learn, as they're often quite motivated to get inside.

2. Encourage your pets to stay in one area of the house (or at least to spend most of their time there) by providing a comfortable bed in a protected corner. Beds (at least their covers) must be removable and washable. If you allow your pets to sleep on their—or your, for that matter—favorite chair, cover it with towels or something else easily washable.

3. Protect and select pet-proof surfaces. Dogs rub against the walls, so paint them a color that can disguise a little dirt and that can be washed a number of times. Pet hair comes off leather furniture effortlessly, whereas many fabrics require you to practically pluck each hair off one at a time. Don't let bird droppings get on any floor or any

furniture at all. Cover anything at risk. For almost any pet—except perhaps a fish—a vacuum with a good rotating beater brush is essential.

4. Feed pets in low-slung, heavy bowls that can't be tipped over. Ditto for water bowls. Put a towel under the bowls. Leave the towel unfolded so it will cover a larger area. Remember to toss the towel into the laundry regularly. By the way, humans tip over pets' water bowls more often than do pets, so put them someplace where that won't happen so often. If you give pets treats, *only* do it in one area—such as in the kitchen—where slobber and droppings are easiest to clean up. In particular, don't feed pets human food at the dining room table. If you do, bits of chicken fat, grease, butter, etc., will continually find their way into your carpet.

5. Give dogs a shower once a month or more often if they start to

smell or when fleas or itching is getting to them—or you. The simplest way to do this (other than than sending them to the doggy "fluff and fold" every other Wednesday, as The Clean Team's venerable Rudy Dinkel does with his overindulged shih tzu) is to install a shower head with a flexible hose. Especially with dogs, keep their claws trimmed to reduce scratches on hardwood and other floors. Ask your vet for a lesson if you haven't done it before.

6. Unless you want to vacuum every day, especially during the seemingly never-ending shedding season, brush dogs and cats every day instead. It's by far the shorter of the two operations, and you'll be amazed and gratified at the amount of hair the brush is picking up. Better in the brush than on the sofa! Not any old brush will work. Too many of them immediately become clogged with hair and are useless from that point on. Especially for short- and medium-length hair, use a rubber horse brush or a metal brush with a serrated blade.

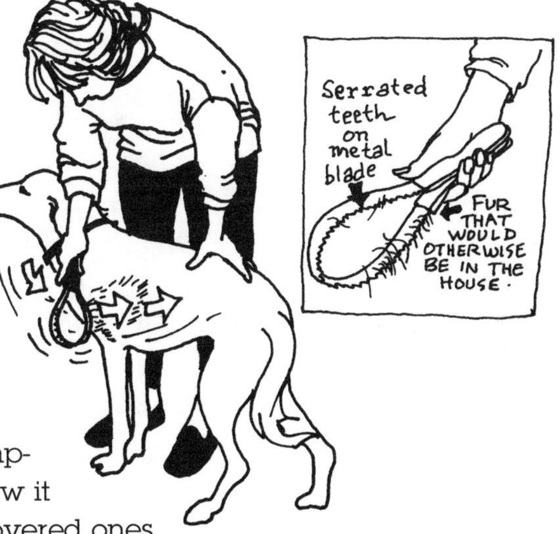

7. Litter boxes (kind of like toilets) are designed to be emptied after use. If the box gets too full, the cat will eschew it and will go somewhere else in your house instead. Covered ones

limit the amount of litter that ends up outside the box. I've noticed self-cleaning ones in the catalogs, but I suspect that proper maintenance, even with that type, is still a daily event.

8. Keep Red Juice, a cleaning "toothbrush" (see Appendix A), and paper towels handy for quick wipe-ups of spills, food droppings, slobber, etc. By the way, check out the slobber habits of the dog breed you're considering living with for its lifetime. With some breeds, that's the hardest maintenance job—and they never outgrow it. (Rule 4 applies: Ask before you buy!)

Pewter

Pewter is susceptible to pitting and staining by acids and other chemicals in foods, so don't leave food on pewter any longer than necessary. Wash right after using. You probably know that it is quite soft for a metal and gets scratched and dented easily. So don't get carried away when polishing it or the piece will deform in your hands.

Pianos

If your piano is important to you, you probably already know to avoid extreme changes in humidity. If you can't avoid these changes, you may need a humidifier or a dehumidifier. Sudden changes in temperature affect both the tone and the wood, so be careful about locating the instrument too close to a heat register, radiator, or window, or either the humidifier or dehumidifier.

If you have them, follow the manufacturer's instructions for cleaning. General guidelines are: If the finish is lacquer (usually black), wipe with an untreated dust cloth. Lacquer finishes are usually not waxed, but you may apply wax to other wood finishes. Heavy dust accumulations can be removed with a brush attachment and the vacuum—very gently, however, because lacquer scratches easily. Also vacuum the keyboard regularly.

Real ivory keys yellow with age. There's nothing you can do about it. Clean them with a cloth dampened with alcohol. (Soap stains ivory.) Modern pianos have plastic (acrylic) keys that can be wiped with a cloth moistened with Red Juice.

Vacuum inside the piano once or twice a year. Use a dusting brush along with a vacuum to catch the dust before it settles further into the piano.

Plants

Dry, Natural, and Artificial Plants. Some folks put dry or silk flower arrangements into place and, since they don't need watering, fertilizing, pruning, or repotting, then forget about them. But they need regular maintenance. Dust them each time you clean. Use a feather duster, a dusting brush, or the brush attachment of the vacuum. However, they can't be maintained in like-new condition. Dried plants break. Brightly colored dry plants will fade no matter what, and will fade rather quickly in the sun. Both will eventually get dirty in spite of regular dusting, and they may or may not look good after washing (*Talking Dirt,* see Appendix B). If you want them to look great for a long time, put them in a glass or plastic display cabinet or box.

Indoor Plants. There are two maintenance concerns. The first is to protect the house and the second is to keep the plant alive. There aren't that many homes without a water ring or some other plant damage somewhere or other. Some good friends of mine have an awful twelve-inch-diameter water stain on their otherwise stunning hardwood floor. My parents' orchid plants have left their mark—literally—on windowsills and on carpets all through the house. This is serious, expensive damage, often requiring refinishing or replacing floors or carpets. Such damage is so common because you usually can't see that a saucer is leaking in the first place, and the leaking water gets trapped under the saucer where it can't escape and evaporate. Thus, the floor surface is kept wet for a long, damaging period of time. Sometimes the leak doesn't start until after you've checked. Or sometimes it seeps through the saucer itself, as with terracotta, so you can't see the leak in any event. Don't let this disheartening damage happen in your home:

1. Use saucers that are 100 percent waterproof and that have ample capacity for excess water. (This usually means plastic.) But don't use inexpensive plastic liners. Use heavy-duty saucers that are unlikely to crack when hit by the vacuum cleaner or otherwise distressed by active household events.
2. Don't put a saucer directly on any surface. Use a wooden trivet available from a nursery or from your kitchen drawer. Avoid metal ones, which will rust. No matter where the trivet comes from or how much it costs, it's worth the price compared to the potential damage you're trying to avoid.
3. Check after the first few waterings to be positive there is no water leaking, seeping, or oozing. Move the plant and lift the saucer and trivet to check. Check again periodically.
4. After each watering, remove standing water from the saucer by pouring it out or using a turkey baster to draw it out.

Excess water is also the most popular way to kill plants because most houseplants left in standing water will die. So don't fill your bathtub with

water and put the houseplants there when you go on vacation. Get either a self-watering pot or some other automatic watering device, or ask the neighbors to water them for you.

Of course, the second most popular way to kill houseplants is to underwater. The best way to water is to put the plant and pot in a sinkful or bucket of water for fifteen minutes or more until the soil is saturated. Remove, allow the water to drain, and replace the plant on its saucer. If plants get severely dried out because of hot weather or skipped waterings, this is about the only way to get the dirt saturated again. A simpler method is simply to water the entire soil surface slowly and thoroughly. After watering, remove any standing water that has collected in the saucer, as just mentioned. Wash the saucers when there is a visible buildup of salts, which can also damage the plant.

Follow fertilizer instructions as it's easy to overfertilize houseplants. Two teaspoons are not better than one. Cut back or stop fertilizing during the winter. Most plants require indirect light but can't take full sun, so unless it's a cactus it is unlikely to survive in a window in the direct sun. Dust plants with a feather duster when you do your routine housecleaning. Wash them occasionally, if possible. It's often easiest to do this outside, but don't leave them in the hot sun to dry for more than a few minutes.

There are two additional maintenance steps for plants. Trim or prune them as needed to remove dead leaves and diseased or damaged shoots, to shape them, or to thin them out. Finally, even though most houseplants like to be fairly tight in their pots, they will eventually become hopelessly root-bound and start to decline. This may take less than a year or up to several years. When it does, you have three choices:

(1) Repot into a larger pot. (2) Remove the plant, trim its roots, and replant in the same pot. (3) Start over again. Option 3 isn't selected nearly often enough in my opinion. Plants have a natural lifespan, and they often don't look all that great during their entire life. You do not have to cling to them until the bitter end. Replace them when they start to look like something you wouldn't even buy at a garage sale, let alone a nursery.

One of the least fussy houseplants is pothos (*Scindapsus*), a viny plant often with attractive variegated leaves. Other low-maintenance plants include most varieties of philodendrons and dracaenas, Chinese evergreen (*Aglaonema modestum*), English ivy (*Hedera helix*), grape ivy (*Cissus rhombifolia*), and India rubber plant (*Ficus elastica*).

Refrigerators

The most important maintenance operation is to keep the condenser coils free of lint, dust, and pet hair. These coils are located either behind the unit (especially in older models) or underneath it. Coils get dirty faster if they are underneath the refrigerator. A heavy accumulation of dust and hair

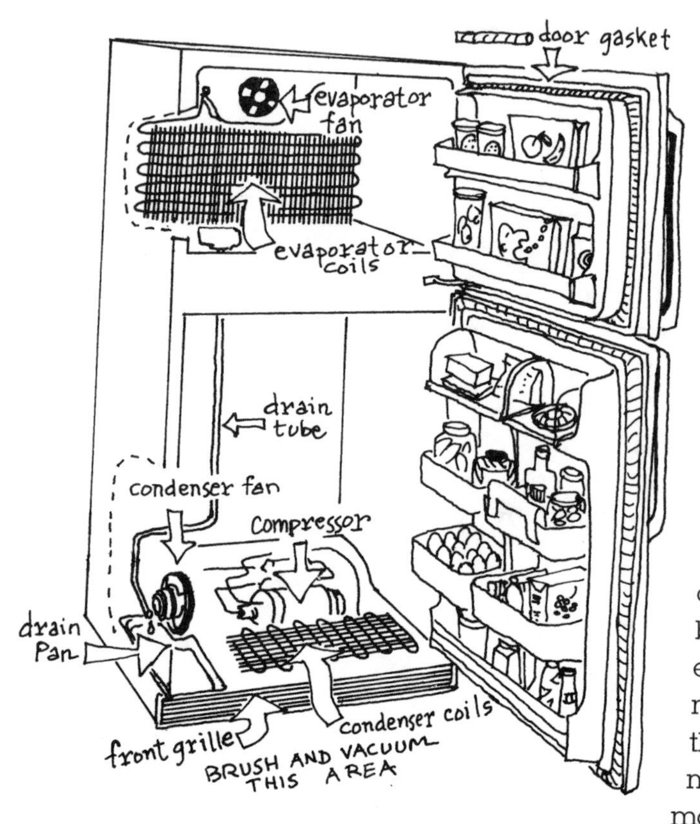

is, unfortunately, an excellent insulator. The refrigerator will continue to run with this extra insulation, but it prevents the coils from dispelling heat. This, in turn, makes the refrigerator run longer. The refrigerator might even run constantly or, if it overheats, fail completely. So if your refrigerator doesn't seem as cold as usual, you've been delivered an early warning that it's past time to clean the coils.

But don't wait for symptoms to develop. Clean the coils regularly. Most manufacturers recommend cleaning them three or four times a year. However, these same manufacturers haven't visited your home, and you may have to clean the coils more or less often than they recommend. The coils in your refrigerator are probably downright filthy now, as they are in just about everyone else's, but clean them right away and mark the date on a calendar. Check on them in three months. If they're still relatively clean, check monthly until there's a buildup. Now you know the maintenance interval for your particular fridge. Indeed, use this same approach when evaluating general maintenance instructions for other appliances.

Finally, even though cats like to sleep in front of the refrigerator's warm air vents, do encourage them to sleep elsewhere or the recleaning interval will shorten by about half.

One good excuse for not cleaning the coils behind the refrigerator is that you can't get at them without moving it. Low wheels can be installed under the refrigerator so you can move it relatively easily. I highly recommend them so your floor won't become adorned with gouges.

The best tool to use is a long-handled brush designed for this job, which looks like a very long bottle brush. It's called a coil or refrigerator brush. Using this brush and the vacuum is the best option, as quite a bit of dust can get stirred up. Use a long-handled brush designed for removing snow from a car's windows, along with the brush attachment on the vacuum if a coil brush is not available. Use the brush attachment and vacuum alone if neither is available. I'm sure you know that, once damaged, these coils

usually can't be fixed by mere mortals, so use caution and be gentle when dusting or vacuuming them.

If the rear-mounted coils are greasy, wash them with warm soapy water. Use towels to catch drip water on other parts of the refrigerator and the floor.

When you move the refrigerator back into place, leave enough space behind it so it's not touching the wall. If the coils are rear-mounted, leave even more room. Most models also require several inches of clearance between the top of the refrigerator and any cupboards above. (Check your manual or call the manufacturer.)

Many newer refrigerators have an "energy-saver" switch that turns off a special type of heater located between the freezer and the refrigerator compartments. Most of us are all in favor of saving energy, so we turn this switch on and don't think of it again—ever. But now the heater is off, and condensation can build up between the compartments. This can result in the growth of mildew and eventually rust. Either don't use the energy-saver option at all (Al Hale suggests it probably only saves a few cents a year!), or go ahead and use it but keep alert for moisture between the freezer and refrigerator compartments. If moisture appears, turn the energy-saver function off.

Keep the gasket that seals the door scrupulously clean. Mold growing on the gasket can make it rot. If a sticky layer starts to pull on the gasket each time the door is opened, the gasket will be pulled out of position. It will eventually tear from being repeatedly stuck and then pulled loose each time the door is opened. Wipe the gasket itself and also wipe where it seals against the refrigerator frame each time you clean the kitchen. If this task is neglected long enough, the gasket can pull itself completely out of position.

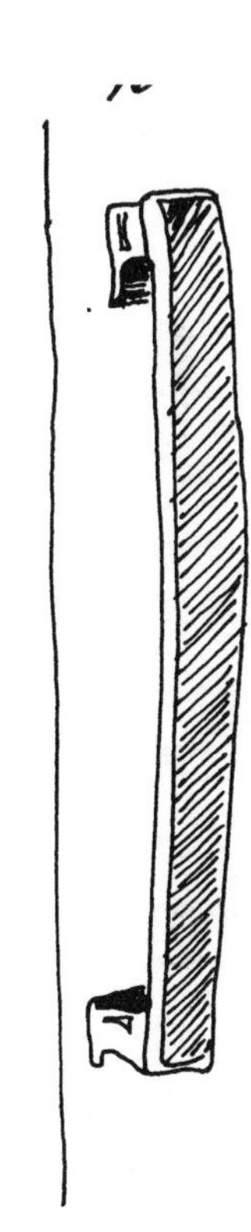

Inspect the gasket visually for tears. Check also for brittleness and cracks. Close the door and check for any obvious gaps. Test to be sure it is sealing properly by closing the door on a dollar bill. There should be tension on the bill as you pull it out slowly.

If the door of your refrigerator doesn't close automatically or if it failed the dollar-bill test, the refrigerator should be tilted back slightly. Do this by having someone tilt the refrigerator back while you adjust the feet or rollers to raise the front just slightly. The idea is to add a little bit of closing force to the door's swing.

If your refrigerator drains to a basin that collects water, the basin must be emptied and cleaned often enough to keep it from overflowing and/or getting funky. Paper bags or towels in a refrigerator are dangerous because they quickly disintegrate, and their remains soon plug up that drain. Indeed, Al Hale refers to paper products as the "silent killers of refrigerators." If there is a drain opening inside the refrigerator, once a year use a turkey baster to force through enough hot water it to keep it clear. If the refrigerator leaks water, something is wrong. Check the drain opening first. If that's not it, call an appliance repair shop.

According to *Reader's Digest New Fix-It-Yourself Manual,* you should check the temperature of both the refrigerator and freezer compartments occasionally. (I'd think that once would be sufficient, unless you suspect that the temperature might have changed.) To perform the test, cool a glass of water in the refrigerator for twenty-four hours. Then put a refrigerator-freezer thermometer (available at houseware- or restaurant-supply stores) in the water. The optimum reading is between 34°F and 40°F. In the freezer, insert the thermometer between two frozen packages. The optimum temperature here is between 0°F and 4°F. Reset the temperature setting(s) as necessary and retest.

Clean the insides of the refrigerator and freezer compartments when they need it. If you routinely clean up spills in the fridge, and if you remember to clean one shelf occasionally as you do your regular housecleaning, a special separate cleaning may never be needed. It's safest to unplug the refrigerator before cleaning it, but since this can often be impractical, just be careful with liquid cleaners around the light, switches, and controls. Use Red Juice and a cleaning cloth. If the fridge smells bad, even after cleaning it, install an open box of baking soda at the back of the top shelf. If necessary, replace every three months (when the season changes). If there is an odor problem in the freezer, do the same thing there.

For most efficient day-to-day operation, don't stuff the refrigerator full. The same is true for the freezer. Air must be able to circulate in both, and they work much harder when overfilled. If you have temporarily overfilled it (e.g., on Thanksgiving Eve), be sure that the door closes completely and the gasket is properly sealed. Don't put things in the refrigerator that don't have to be there. In particular, check condiments to be sure they have to be refrigerated. If you have seven partially full containers of various mustards, some of which date back to your bell-bottom era, ask yourself how many more years you want to pay to refrigerate them.

If you're leaving home for a long vacation, eat or give away the food in the refrigerator. Unplug, clean, dry thoroughly, and leave the door ajar so air can circulate. Food that spoils while you're on vacation may grow mold and mildew and create odors that penetrate the refrigerator's insulation so deeply that the only solution is to discard the refrigerator entirely. For shorter vacations, use up the perishable food but leave the refrigerator on. In either case, manually turn off the icemaker water line and lift the arm on the icemaker to stop its operation.

Remote Controls

If you get in the habit of laying remote controls upside-down after each use, they'll stay cleaner longer. And if someone does manage to spill something on one, it's less likely to be damaged. Vacuum them with the brush attachment when you do your normal vacuuming. Clean battery contacts with a pencil eraser every few months—or at least when you put in new batteries.

Security Systems

The burglar alarm system is so important that I recommend having your alarm company perform an annual inspection. They can test the door and window sensors, motion detectors, glass-break sensors, tamper switches, and backup batteries, and clean the smoke detectors.

If doing it yourself, one of the most important tests is to be sure that all the circuits to the sensors at doors and windows are working. Your owner's manual can help you, but one way is to open a door or window with a sensor and check that a light is displayed at the control panel. This is accomplished a lot more easily by two people yelling back and forth rather than one person traipsing back and forth.

Avoid false alarms by practicing until everyone knows how to use the system. Purchase wireless "keys" that allow you to arm and disarm it if someone in the household has trouble operating it without triggering a false alarm.

Septic Systems

Properly maintained, a modern septic system will last twenty years or more. But with just the right sort of neglect, you can manage to destroy one in short order. The cost of replacement, especially if local codes have changed since it was originally installed (and they've changed considerably in many areas), can be staggering. Replacement or repair construction can also wreak havoc on other expensive things like landscaping, driveways, and sidewalks.

Here are some steps you must take on a day-to-day basis to make sure your septic tank functions properly—at least until you move. The first step is simple, if a bit annoying: Don't use your garbage disposer. Get rid of garbage the old-fashioned way—in the garbage can. Okay, you can run small amounts of debris through the disposer to help keep the sink from clogging. And if your mother-in-law uses it steadily when she visits, it won't necessarily doom the septic tank. Otherwise, practice great restraint. It's not that the bacteria in the septic tank won't dissolve this waste pretty much the same as they do the human waste in there; it's just

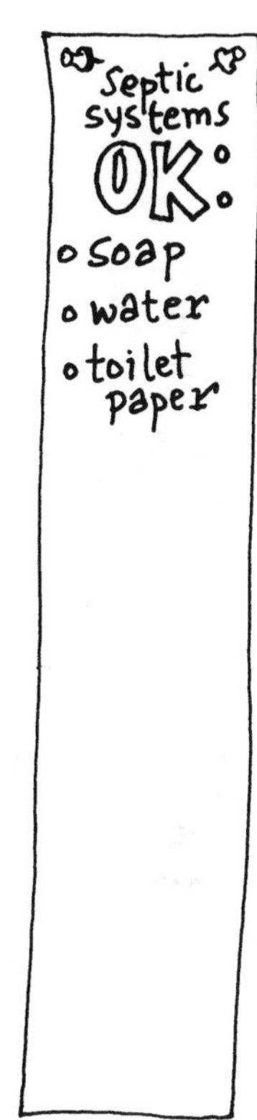

that the extra garbage-disposer material can overload and/or overfill it before its time—in as little as a couple of years, from what I've read.

You shouldn't pour grease into a sink in any event, but be particularly careful of grease getting into the septic system. Grease is not easily broken down by the bacteria, and it plugs up leach lines. As you know, paint, varnish, polyurethane, gasoline, oil, paint thinner, pesticides, antifreeze, and the like are all off-limits to the septic system. Ditto for paper towels, disposable diapers, napkins, and tissues (i.e., all paper except toilet paper), plastic products, rubber products, and cloth. Likewise, no sanitary napkins or tampons. Here's an easy summary: Don't put anything other than the effluent from sinks, toilets, and washing machines into the septic system.

It's unwise to flush large amounts of water into the septic system in a short period of time. So, for example, try to space out bouts of laundry. Since the washing machine is a major contributor to water volume entering the septic system, the next time you replace your washing machine you might consider choosing a front-loading machine, which uses only a fraction of the water that a top-loader does. Several American manufacturers have only recently released full-size front-loaders.

For septic systems, it's extra important to fix any leaking toilets or other fixtures that are continually adding water to the system. If you don't get around to fixing a leak right away, at least turn off the water supply to the leak in the meantime.

Whether or not to regularly use enzyme additives is an open question. They are intended to increase the bacterial population that breaks down solid waste in the septic system. They can't hurt the system, but the U.S. Department of Health, Education, and Welfare's *Manual of Septic Tank Practice* reports that none of the dozens of products on the market have proven to be an advantage in properly controlled tests. More important is preventive maintenance: limiting the types of waste and the amount of water you put into the system.

Have a septic system inspected right after moving into a used home unless a septic inspection was part of the presale building inspection. You can wait up to four years with a new home. Then ask the inspector when and how often it should be emptied. It's possible that it will need pumping more often, especially if the tank is undersized; more likely, you will find that you need not pump it more than once every five years or so.

Showerheads

If you have naturally soft water or have a water softener, no maintenance is required. But hard water eventually stops up showerheads, often so slowly that you don't really notice. Keep them running freely by soaking overnight in a 50 percent vinegar and water solution on a preventive basis. This can be accomplished without removing the showerhead. Put the vinegar solution into a plastic bag and tape it over the showerhead overnight.

Showers See **Bathtubs.**

Silver

If you want to find out about silver, go to Gump's in San Francisco. It's easy to get slightly intoxicated by the beauty of the Buccellati and other silver services there, but we managed to complete an interrogation of their exceedingly patient and knowledgeable silver specialist.

The two biggest care issues for silver are cleaning and storage. As for cleaning, the procedure is governed by the unavoidable fact that silver is a soft metal with a vulnerable finish. Accordingly, it's almost obligatory to wash and polish good silver (or any silver you are fond of) by hand. Forget about silly schemes involving aluminum foil and chemical baths in the kitchen sink.

Is the dishwasher safe? The simple answer is no. In addition to being exposed to harsh dishwasher detergent, the silver may knock against other metal items or be stained by food inside the dishwasher. It's far better to wash silver in hot soapy water as soon after use as possible, and then dry the pieces by hand immediately afterward. Polish is not needed every time you clean a piece.

When it comes time to polish, the brand is not all that critical, although you should avoid abrasive polishes and those that claim to work instant miracles through modern chemistry. Don't rub too zealously: you may also remove a dark patina or finish that was deliberately applied or that gives the silver much of its depth and warmth.

Careful storage is particularly important for silver, because an oversight in this regard can do serious damage. The great enemies of stored silver are rubber, salt, moisture, and the sulfur fumes given off by many foods as they ripen. One of the more practical storage solutions is a treated cloth storage bag. You can make your own (buy flannel treated for silver storage—*not* regular flannel—at a fabric store) or buy them ready-made at places like Gump's (1-800-444-0450).

When all is said and done, one of the best things you can do with silver it to *use it*. What's the point of having a fine piece of silver if you stuff it away in the closet? Besides, regular handling will create that fine luster and patina that are so prized in silver.

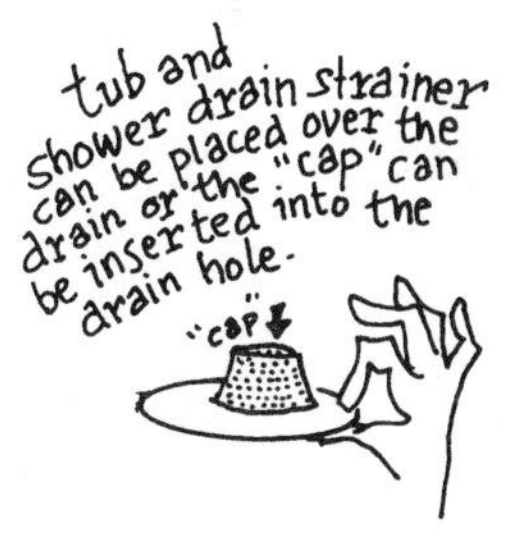

Sinks

Thou Shalt Not Pour Grease Down Kitchen Drains. Pour it instead into an empty can and store it in the refrigerator until it's solidified or the can is full. Then put the can into a plastic zippered bag (or one sealed with a rubber band) before depositing it in the trash.

In sinks, tubs, or showers where hair is washed, use a plastic or metal hair strainer or screen to help keep most hair out of the drain. Quite possibly the only civilized purpose served by a used cotton swab is to twirl it around in the screen to remove accumulated hair.

Don't let a small sliver of a soap bar get into the drain. It's worth 3 cents, but can cost you a $300 plumber's bill if it gets stuck in the trap.

Porcelain Sinks. Scraping metal utensils or pots against porcelain will ingratiate you only to sink suppliers. Plastic mats will help protect sinks from scratches and stains caused by pots and pans. They also provide some protection from accidental breakage while washing dishes.

Acids will etch sinks if allowed to remain, so rinse away the remains of acidic foods like lemons, cranberries, tomatoes, and vinegar. Tannins in coffee and tea create difficult-to-remove stains in short order. It's a good idea not to let any food debris accumulate in the sink. Either run it through the disposer or put in the garbage. On the other end of the pH scale, strong alkalis such as household bleach also attack porcelain, so use sparingly and rinse well. The same is true for photographic supplies. Don't use a sink to hold any photographic or developer solutions unless you're willing to live with the resulting stains.

It happens all the time, so I suppose it bears repeating: Don't use the sink as a handy spot to store tools, paint cans, and so on, when you're redecorating or attacking some other household project. Hammers are dropped and permanent nicks are created. Why tempt fate? Cover sinks and other fixtures before projects get under way.

Stainless Steel Sinks. For starters, don't even try to maintain the brushed finish or the cute little swirls or grain lines created by the manufacturing process. That would only drive you crazy because it's not humanly possible. I suppose you could preserve them for a year or two if you washed the sink with nothing but stainless steel cleaner and a soft cloth. I much prefer to wash them with whatever is used to wash the other sinks in the house.

As with porcelain sinks (page 154), mats will cut down on marks caused when washing pots, cutlery, and pans. Stainless steel sinks are particularly vulnerable to scratches from green cleaning pads, so don't even think of using them on this type of sink.

Smoke Detectors

Blow out dust with canned air once a year (more often if you live in a dusty area or have had false alarms in spite of annual maintenance). First remove the cover, and aim the canned air as best you can to blow dust away from the middle of the detector. How-

ever, no matter which way you aim the air blast, the dust particles can easily trigger a false alarm. So especially if you're perched on a ladder, it's wise to be mentally prepared for the possibility that the alarm may commence blasting. Don't let it blast you off the ladder. A pair of earplugs is a good idea. (And, of course, forewarn your cohabitants and read up on how to shut the thing off if it activates.) At the same time, check or automatically replace batteries of detectors not hard-wired into the household current. If there's a chance you won't remember to change the batteries, make a maintenance schedule book that lists the different activities that must be done. This is not an optional maintenance chore, yet you read every year about entire families wiped out in a fire in a house equipped with smoke detectors, but detectors with dead batteries.

Speakers

According to Franklynn Peterson, in his book *How to Fix Damn Near Everything,* the single most common ailment in listening systems of all sorts—stereos, transistor radios, and even TVs—is a bad connection caused by corrosion, loose wires, or wear. That being the case, maintenance should be geared to protecting these connections from danger. Start off by installing wires correctly. San Francisco audio expert Lewis

Downs reminds us to leave enough slack in wires so components can be moved to clean around and under without straining the connections. But it's not a good idea to have too much excess wire. Especially if the excess wire is arranged in a coil, it could turn into something like an antenna. Don't pull plugs out by the wire; pull on the plug itself. Don't let wires or other connections get damp, and don't locate them where they are in even the slightest danger of getting wet. Use the best wires and connectors you can afford. Besides creating future maintenance problems (see Rule 3), low-quality wires can pick up hum and interference. Don't hook up additional speakers unless you know what you're doing. If you do it wrong, you could end up with no speakers at all.

It doesn't hurt to remove a speaker's grille cloth and frame (it usually snaps on and off) to vacuum inside the speaker and both sides of the fabric. Just be gentle with the paper-thin speaker membrane. If the cat (or anything else, for that matter) ruins the speaker fabric, replace it with loosely woven "sound transparent" cloth available at stereo or electronics stores. Most contemporary speakers have no wood in the cabinet surface (it's vinyl), so furniture polish isn't really necessary. Just wipe with Red Juice and a cloth. Polish it only if you want to add shine.

Steamers and Rice Cookers

Other than washing them after use, the most important maintenance issue involves nearby items. Don't use steamers or cookers directly below kitchen cabinets because moist air can be trapped underneath the cabinets and eventually cause mischief—usually in the form of black mildew.

Stone Building Materials

Mother Nature was kind enough to provide natural stone building materials that are stunning and original works of art. To protect and preserve these beautiful and costly materials, preventive maintenance steps are critical but not complicated. Here are four considerations:

1. Contrary to what we may think, and even though the physical properties of various natural stones vary widely, they are all absorbent—even granite. So they will all soak up water, and if the water contains dirt, the dirt will end up inside small fissures in the stone and permanently darken or stain it. Many stone surfaces will soak up oils with similar dire consequences.
2. Polished stone, until recently the most popular choice of consumers, has a highly reflective surface that allows it to show off more of the unique color, grain, and contrasts that make the stone so beautiful.

That glass-like polished surface is also correspondingly vulnerable to scratches and chemical damage that can make it look dull, white, or lifeless. Reduce ongoing maintenance by selecting less highly polished finishes on floors (e.g., "flamed," a rough finish) and counters (e.g., "honed," a smooth but not glass-like finish). Honed finish in particular is becoming increasingly popular. It still shows off the beauty of the stone but requires less upkeep.

3. Some natural stones (marble and limestone, for example) are vulnerable to acids, including very mild acids like those found in many soft drinks, oranges, lemons, and tomatoes, or even fingerprints.

4. Hard water can be very damaging to natural stone. If your home has hard water, and stone was installed inside the tub/shower areas, you'd be wise to install a water softener.

Maintenance requirements depend on the type of stone (slate vs. granite, for example) as well as its use (marble as a bathroom counter or a kitchen floor, for example). Stone is a natural product, and as such its properties vary widely: even two different marbles may have widely different properties. Before you make a purchase, ask about specific properties (especially weaknesses) that could increase maintenance efforts. For example, one tile expert told us that green marble is not suited for installation in wet locations, whereas other types of marble are less vulnerable to moisture. Here are three specific maintenance steps:

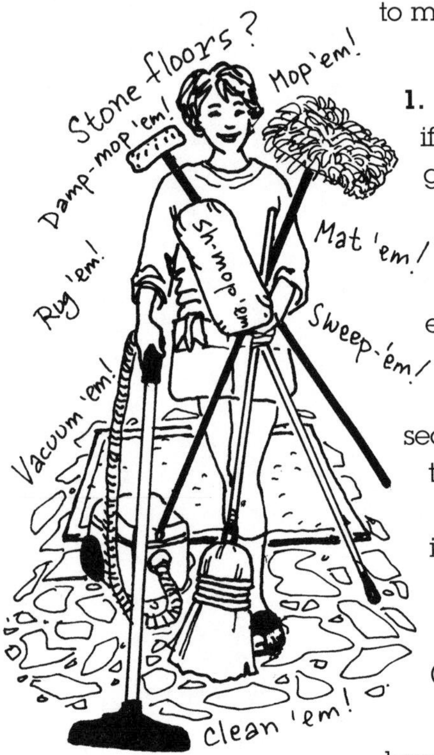

1. Seal the stone. This can actually be done before installation, but if not, wait one to two weeks after installation until the stone and grout are completely dry. Use a penetrating or impregnating sealant that will repel both water and oil. Don't use a surface sealant that just coats the surface. Select a sealant that will not alter the color or change the gloss of the surface unless that's the effect you want. Therefore, it's vital that you make a complete test—usually on a representative sample of stone—to be sure. Some sealants require a second coat right away, and most sealants should be reapplied once a year or so to maintain full protection. A number of good sealants are on the market. Consult a local stone dealer or even a home-supply store for help in choosing among them.

2. Avoid using an acrylic floor finish on natural stone, as it can add a plastic or artificial look. If additional protection is desired (besides sealing it), use wax.

3. Keep it clean. The secret of beautiful natural stone is mainly to keep it clean after sealing. Complicated cleaning agents, maintenance procedures, or restoration steps will never be needed if the surface is cleaned regularly. Abrasions and stains, especially on floors, will take their toll if cleanliness is not maintained. Mats are particularly important. Use nonslip mats or rugs. Vacuum, sweep, dust-mop, and/or damp-mop daily, if necessary. Regular washing with a natural soap (not a detergent) such as Murphy's Oil Soap or Ivory Liquid not only cleans but also enhances the appearance of many types of natural stone, and helps seal it. A specialized stone soap (available at hardware stores and stone dealers) is also recommended. Because stone absorbs liquids, change dirty mop water often, rinse the mop often, and rinse the floor after washing. Dry the floor if streaks remain after rinsing.

Use coasters or other protection on countertops or tables. Be vigilant about spills (remember, lemonade and anything else even slightly acidic will etch marble and some other stone surfaces), and wipe them up right away. Wet again with water and wipe a second time to remove any traces of acid.

If your shower is lined with natural stone, and hard water is prevalent in your area, the regular use of a squeegee to wipe standing water from the shower walls is mandatory. Don't use an acidic cleaner (Tile Juice included) to remove hard-water spots. Any nonacidic cleaner that works for you is fine.

Granite. It will absorb oil and water, so it usually should be sealed, but it is harder than most other stone and is resistant to food acids. This makes it a favorite choice for kitchen counters.

Limestone. It has the same weaknesses as **Marble,** below.

Marble. Polished marble requires careful maintenance when used as a floor (it's easily scratched), or as a kitchen countertop (it's absorbent and vulnerable to acids). In addition to applying a sealer, consider using paste wax (liquid or solid) for extra protection when marble serves as flooring or when installed in the kitchen for any purpose. **Note:** If you're considering a purchase, marble is not recommended for either place. Polished marble is more suited for vertical surfaces, and granite is superior for horizontal surfaces in the kitchen.

Slate. Slate is softer than most natural stones and is thereby fairly easily scratched. But it's still quite durable, and the wear is concentrated on the high spots of its textured surface. If a reflective look is desired, select a sealer or wax that will produce one.

Stains on natural stones are more thoroughly explored in *Talking Dirt,* but here's an overview: Start by washing well with dish soap and water or by spraying and wiping with Red Juice. If that isn't effective, try removing oily stains (grease, butter, cream, etc.) with alcohol. For tannin or dye stains (coffee, tea, soft drinks, etc.) use 12 percent hydrogen peroxide (hair-bleaching strength) straight out of the bottle. When using hydrogen peroxide on dark stone, test first. Stubborn or deep stains will require the application of a poultice (see *Talking Dirt*, Appendix B, for the thrilling details).

Storage Areas

Don't store valuable possessions in the far reaches of your home for months or years on end without checking on them occasionally. Check once after a couple of months, and then once a year or so. Attic storage is subject to extremes of hot and cold, so don't store anything there that could be damaged by such violent changes in temperature. If there are louvers or vents in the attic, they were deliberately installed to allow warm moist air to escape. Don't cover them. Basement storage may encourage mildew growth, even inside boxes. Put desiccants inside the boxes, if needed. Whether it's the attic, basement, garage, or closet, creatures such as spiders, bugs, and even mice will move in soon after the activity of bringing in the items dies down. Check after a few months of storage, and add mothballs, repackage, or move the items to solve any problems.

Stoves

Stoves should be level so that flames burn uniformly, pilot lights work properly, and the oven doesn't produce lopsided desserts! If you moved your stove for any reason, recheck to be sure that it's level when you put it back into place. Nearly all stoves have a built-in adjustment pod at each corner.

Stove Tops, Enamel. To make a stove top last and to keep it working efficiently, use the lowest temperature possible for each cooking procedure. The drip trays under burners also serve as reflector bowls. They reflect heat back up where it's needed for cooking. High heat can crack or permanently stain the enamel on reflectors and make them less efficient. Plain old food spills can also make permanent stains, so proper care also includes keeping these drip trays clean. When cooking, use a big enough pot or pan to provide enough head space to avoid spills and boil-overs. Wipe up any spills as soon as practicable. As my aunt Ruth used to say, "The cookder they get, the harder they are to remove." It's okay to move hot pots directly from a burner to the stove top because the porcelain enamel can take the heat. But since the porcelain can be scratched, it's even safer to move the pot to a trivet, spider, or different burner instead.

It's not a good idea to cover or wrap the drip trays with aluminum foil.

This can trap heat and make the drip trays overheat or even melt. Use store-bought liners instead.

If you've led a charmed life, the metal trim, the drip pans, the broiler pan, and the oven racks will all fit into the dishwasher. If so, maintain these items with minimal effort by popping them into the dishwasher occasionally. Don't ignore the knobs like ninety out of a hundred people do when cleaning. Red Juice and a toothbrush will keep them looking like new. **Note:** Speaking of knobs, sometimes their painted marks wear off so you can't tell high from low, or they get pulled off the stove by little hands. Ditto for metal trim around burners, drip pans, and so forth. These parts can be replaced via GE's Parts Master Program—usually whether your appliance is GE or not. Spruce up old appliances with new knobs, trim rings, and so forth. Replace filthy appliance filters, pumps, switches, and valves if you're so inclined. Have the appliance's brand name and model number handy, and call 1-800-626-2002 (see Appendix B). If the part is available, you can order it and have it shipped directly to you, or they can tell you where to get the part in your area. Lots of big cities have appliance parts stores as well.

Stove Tops, Smooth Ceramic Glass or Black Glass. The important maintenance concern with glass stove tops is that they are susceptible to scratches and stains. Dirty or wet pots can burn a stain right into a stove top. Pans made of soft metal (such as lighter-weight aluminum pans) can rub off on the harder glass surface, leaving gray or black marks.

To keep glass stove tops in best shape, follow these simple suggestions: Use clean and dry pans when cooking; lift rather than slide pans when moving them; clean the stovetop (after it has cooled sufficiently) after each use with a soapy sponge or a white pad and a paper towel; wipe spills immediately after they occur if you can safely do so; and finally, try to prevent spills by using large enough pots and pans and leaving plenty of headroom for boiling and stirring.

Stove Hoods

Clean the inside of the hood regularly. If you let grease build up, not only is the hood a chore to clean, but it becomes less efficient at attracting grease to the vent. Grease that isn't drawn into the vent settles on other surfaces throughout the kitchen and the house. (Take a quick look up under there and imagine that stuff settling on your couch, for example.) Wash the inside of the hood with a clear ammonia/water solution (25% or more ammonia) and water or Red Juice. Use a brush or white pad if there is a buildup of grease (also see **Fans, Exhaust or Vent**).

Teakettles

As in coffeemakers, mineral deposits will form inside a teakettle if you have hard water in your area. To remove this buildup, combine equal parts of water and white vinegar, and fill to the normal water line. Bring to a boil, remove from heat, and let sit until cool. Rinse well. Repeat if necessary. It helps if you empty the kettle after each use rather than leaving it partially full of water all the time.

Telephone, Cordless

To maintain proper charging of the all-important batteries, periodically clean the charge contacts on the handset and base with a pencil eraser. If the charge doesn't seem to last very long, try running the battery all the way down before recharging.

Cordless phones will have less interference if not located next to heating appliances and devices that generate electrical noise (for example, TVs, motors, power lines, other telephones, and fluorescent lamps). If an appliance causes interference, move the phone base to a different electrical circuit. Moving the base upstairs often improves reception also.

Vacuum the telephone keys with the brush attachment when you are doing your regular housecleaning. Remove fingerprints and dirt by wiping with a Red Juice–dampened cloth.

Telephone Answering Devices

My experience has been that there's little you can do to maintain these machines. They quit working soon after the expiration of their warranty, and they cannot be fixed—only replaced with a sparkling new, unimproved, more expensive model.

For your illumination (it isn't maintenance), San Francisco audio expert Lewis Downs swears that you can improve the audio quality of the outgoing message, in spite of the tiny and cheap microphones being used these days, by doing the following: Drape a towel over your head and hover close to the microphone during the recording session (just don't let anyone take a picture of you doing so). We tested it, and he's right. It *does* work.

Televisions

Protect your TV by plugging it into a surge protector.

Ask any repairman and you'll hear horror stories about what they find in TVs, stereos, VCRs, and so forth. Roaches, geckos, dead flies by the score, coins, mountains of dust, spilled soda, animal fur, and urine (usually from a cat), to name a few. Keep food and drink away from the unit entirely to avoid spills as well as to avoid attracting uninvited insect and mammalian visitors. If you can't control the dust or the cat, place a cloth over the set when it's not in use (after it has cooled off) and/or install an air cleaner nearby. Install the TV in an enclosed cabinet if you can, but if the back of the cabinet is sealed, keep the doors open after use to dissipate residual heat.

The picture tube needs cleaning occasionally to remove the never-ending buildup of dust that's electrostatically attracted to it. When you're doing your routine vacuuming in the area, use the brush attachment to remove 99 percent of the dust. While you're at it, vacuum the knobs and any cooling vents you can reach. A light spray with Blue Juice and a swipe with a cleaning cloth will finish the job. Don't use any liquid cleaner on projection screens or screens that aren't perfectly smooth. Just vacuum or dry-wipe only. **Note:** I've been told that Endust acts as an antistatic product to help cut down on the amount of dust that's attracted to electronic stuff—for example, the dust that's always on your TV screen.

Termites

Termites are attracted to wood in any event, but small leaks or drips that make wood and the dirt below it wet will create a hugely inviting welcome mat—and convenient entry point—for the nasty little critters. (Moisture also attracts hordes of other bugs and pests, not to mention encouraging the start of dry rot, but let's not get sidetracked on those cheery subjects, shall we?) Order a termite inspection for your home annually. The damage that termites can cause is so great compared to the cost of an inspection that it's a critical maintenance step. Look in the Yellow Pages for an inspector (licensed, if appropriate in your state). In states such as California, pest control reports are public documents available to anyone who asks for a copy. The idea is that if a swarm of winged or crawling creatures is invading the neighborhood, you have a right to know. If you see a "Ted the Termite Terminator" van parked in front of the neighbor's house, ask him what's going on, or go to City Hall to get a copy of the report if the two of you haven't spoken since he ran over your garbage cans seventeen years ago.

If you live in a known termite zone (practically anywhere, unfortunately), you can go a step further and hire exterminators to treat the perimeter of your home on a preventive basis. If you want to do inspections yourself, a number of good do-it-yourself books are available, such as *The Virgin Homeowner* by Janice Papolos and *The Complete*

Guide to Four Season Home Maintenance by Dave Heberle and Richard Scutella.

Thermostats

Remove the thermostat cover once a year or so. It usually twists off if round and folds down if rectangular. Carefully vacuum or blow out accumulated dust and lint with canned air from an electronics or video store. (Do this task at the same time you clean the smoke detectors, since both jobs call for a blast of canned air.)

Replace batteries in programmable thermostats once a year.

Toasters and Toaster Ovens

If you remove the crumbs after each use, a good toaster or toaster oven can last a lifetime. After the appliance cools and just before you put it away, either remove the crumb tray and empty it or turn it upside-down and shake the crumbs out. Or use a dusting brush to loosen the crumbs and then shake them out. Wipe the crumb tray with a damp cloth occasionally. If your toaster smokes despite this regimen, there are probably a few doesn't-quite-fit-unless-you-really-push-it bagel scrapings and pop-tart tailings stuck on the heating elements. Once the appliance has cooled and been unplugged, *gently* loosen and remove these scrapings with a toothbrush. Keep an eye on the condition of the cord and plug—especially if the appliance is more than a few years old. Test it after use by running it through an empty toast cycle three times. Then check the plug and cord to see if they're hot. If they are, you should have the cord replaced.

Remove burned-on globs and melted-on plastic bags from the outside of chrome toasters with a razor blade (in a razor holder) and Red Juice. Spray the area with Red Juice and hold the razor at a low angle to avoid scratching the finish. Only the lightest of pressure is needed. Finish up by spraying with a glass cleaner such as Blue Juice and wiping dry to leave a streak-free surface.

Don't try to turn a toaster oven into a full-size oven. Use it to warm things, to bake small items such as potatoes, to cook frozen dinners, and so on. Wash racks in soap and water or in the dishwasher, but not in a self-cleaning oven.

Toilets

Toilets can and, therefore, eventually will leak in a variety of places. The good news is that the replacement parts—at least if the toilet isn't more than twenty or so years old—usually cost only a few dollars. Despite protestations about not being a do-it-yourselfer, I make an exception when the parts are this cheap—and plumbers so far in the other direction.

And don't worry, this won't put the plumbers out of business. We'll all need them for other, far graver emergencies sooner or later.

Occasionally a suspected leak may only be condensation dripping from the tank to the floor. Wipe the tank dry to see if this stops the leak. The most common leaks in a toilet don't make water drip where you can see it. One leak is the type that you become aware of when water is heard continuing to run long after the toilet was flushed. Most of us "fix" this problem by jiggling the flush handle. This leak is caused by the tank ball or flapper not seating properly. Jiggling the handle maneuvers the ball or flap into a tighter fit on the valve seat and so prevents the water from draining out. To correct this type of leak, the lift chain may have to be moved to a different setting on the flush handle so the tank ball or flapper will settle squarely onto the valve seat on its own. By the way, if the toilet doesn't flush at all and the handle doesn't have any resistance when you touch it, the culprit is probably that lift chain. It has become separated from the flush handle and simply needs to be reattached.

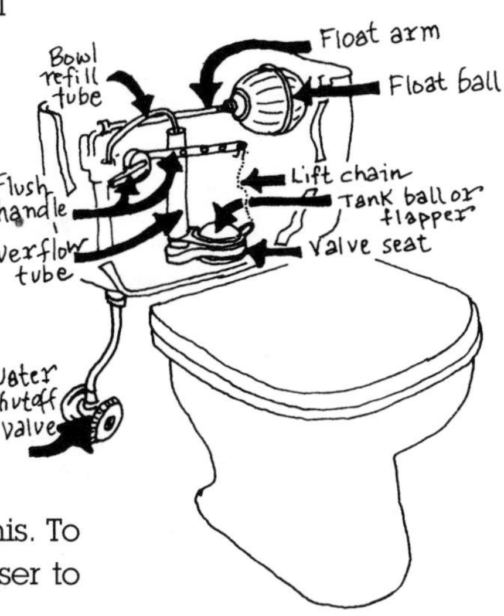

Another common leak happens when water continues to run into the overflow tube after the tank is full and the float ball is all the way up. (Lift the tank lid and look.) Jiggling the handle won't stop this. To fix this type of leak, bend the float arm so that the float will be closer to the bottom of the tank.

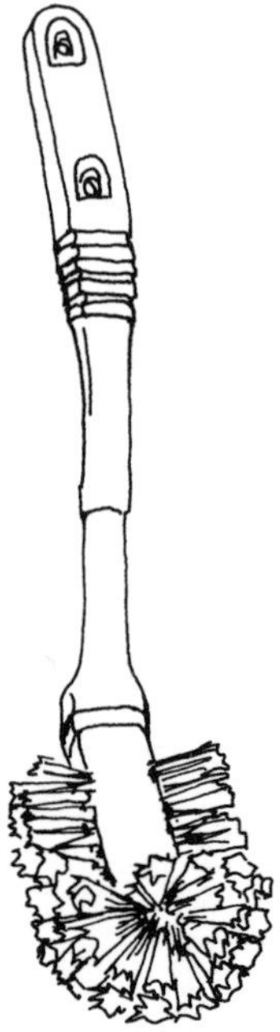

A third type of leak becomes apparent when the water comes on for a few seconds every so often for no apparent reason. This is also caused by water leaking between the tank ball and the valve seat. First try correcting it by cleaning both of these parts. Turn off the shutoff valve (clockwise turn) and flush the toilet. Clean both parts where they meet by wiping with a cleaning cloth or white pad. If this doesn't solve the problem, get replacement parts.

It's safest to take the old tank ball or flapper with you to the store. I recently replaced my six-year-old tank ball and *no* tools were required. I bought plastic parts that could be removed and installed by hand. I picked up two sets while I was there (they were less than five dollars each) to save myself another trip sometime in the future. I don't know if that was such a great idea. Now I'm sort of looking forward to another toilet having the same problem.

If a toilet threatens to overflow, first turn the water off. Then quickly remove the tank lid and press down on the tank ball or stopper to prevent water in the tank from getting into the overflowing bowl. This is a drainage problem and requires a plunger, snake, or plumber (see **Drains**).

Wire brushes can leave black marks on porcelain that are difficult to remove (use cleanser and a white pad), so I recommend all-plastic toilet brushes for everyday cleaning.

New low-flow toilets use less water but do a worse job of flushing.

Make sure yours is using as much water as it was designed for by removing the lid and checking the water level. If it should hold more water, bend the rod that supports the float (the metal or plastic ball) upward. Even if the water amount is correct, if you flush disposable diapers in a low-flow toilet, faithfully follow the directions that come with the diapers or you will surely plug the toilet. If you continue to hold the handle down for a few seconds after the flush, you'll get a somewhat more effective flush—a "superflush," as I believe it's called. (Don't do this every time because it uses more water.) In any event, keep a plunger on hand because you'll probably need it—see **Drains.**

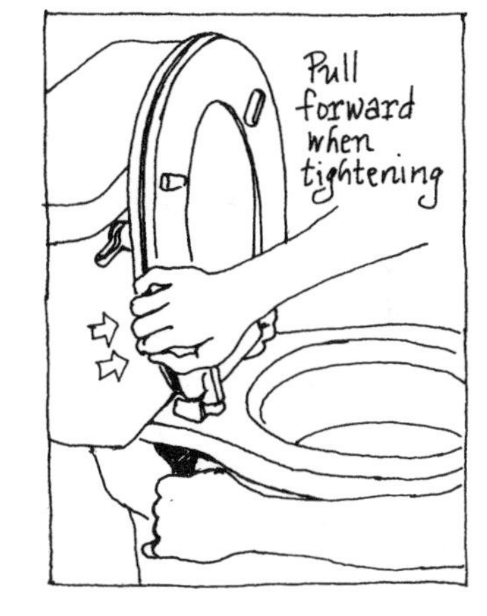

Toilet Seats

The hinges will eventually start to rust—especially if the seat was cheap to begin with and if it wasn't cleaned properly and regularly. Faithfully clean hinges—along with the other toilet surfaces—with Red Juice and a toothbrush. By cleaning the hinges with a toothbrush, you will remove any remnants of urine that encourage rust. Wipe with a cleaning cloth.

When replacing the toilet seat, get the type that attaches to the toilet with plastic bolts because they make both installation and future removal simpler. First remove the old seat, which can be difficult if bolts are rusted and frozen. If they are, apply penetrating oil (place paper towels to catch drips) and let it sit overnight. The next day use a long-handled wrench, if available, to add leverage. Don't hit the bolts or the wrench with a hammer: the toilet is like glass. As a last resort, a hacksaw may be necessary. Clean the newly exposed area well, using a white pad and Red Juice. While tightening the mounting bolts, pull forward on the new seat and cover. If the seat is pushed all the way back when it is tightened, it may not stay up when lifted because it will hit the toilet tank lid at the wrong angle.

Trash Compactors

Other than keeping the compactor clean, the secret to long life is to compact correctly or not to compact at all. Here's a list of things not to compact (it seems pretty obvious, but you never know): paint, lacquer, paint thinner, kerosene and other flammables, aerosol cans, insecticides, fireworks, and ammunition. Don't compact things that aren't empty such as hairspray in a pump spray container, iodine, and so forth. If you don't recycle glass, you can compact it by placing it on its side on top of other garbage, keeping it away from the sides of the compactor.

Remove the entire drawer every six months or so and check behind it. Most drawers can be removed by pulling them out and then lifting up. Pick up the debris that has collected here, and then spray and wipe the area. Wash the drawer and replace it.

TVs See **Televisions.**

Vacation Maintenance Checklist

Going on vacation for a week or more? Here's a short list of things for you to do before you leave. The idea is to help you relax and not worry about what you might have forgotten to do. You're on your own about stopping mail and newspaper delivery, and turning off the coffeepot.

1. Turn down the water heater to the vacation setting (see **Water Heaters**).
2. Turn off the hot- and cold-water supplies to the washing machine (see **Washing Machines**).
3. Depending on the length of your vacation, empty the refrigerator either completely or partially (see **Refrigerators**).
4. Turn off the water supply to the automatic ice-maker (see **Refrigerators**).
5. Turn the water softener to the "bypass" mode.
6. Pour enzyme drain cleaner into slow drains (see **Drains**).
7. If you can get a relative or neighbor to help with access, this is a great time to have the carpets shampooed (see **Carpets and Rugs**).

8. Especially if neighbors or relatives are coming over to feed the cat or water the plants anyway, also have them check to be sure the power to the freezer is on each time they're in your home.

Vacuum Cleaners

Overfilling the dust bag can actually cause dirt to be beaten back into the carpet! That's because when the bag is overfilled, it doesn't work as efficiently and can't pick up the dirt. It just whips it in and out of the vacuum's beater head a few times as you pass over an area with the machine. Most vacuums also suffer a decrease in suction performance, and many start to spew more dust back into the air. So replace the vacuum bag when it's only three-quarters full. Allowing the bag to get completely full doesn't

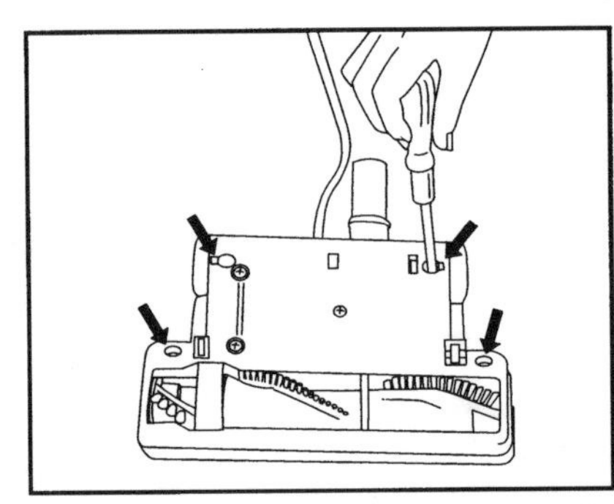

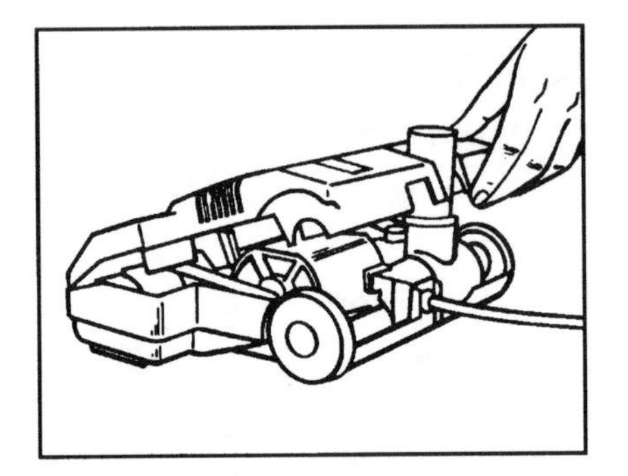

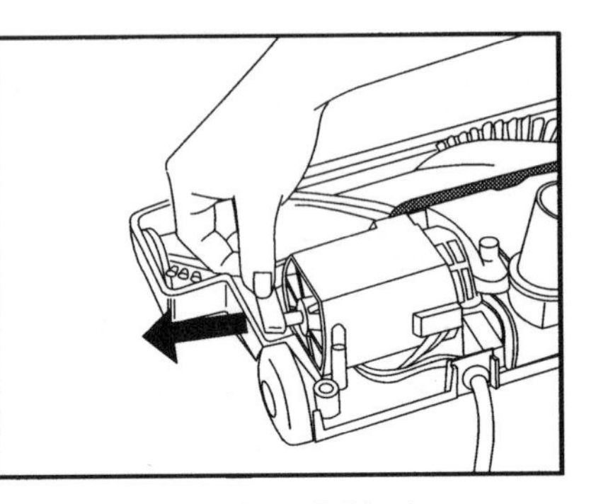

Illustrations courtesy of The Hoover Company, who reminds us to "Always disconnect cord from electric outlet before servicing the [vacuum] cleaner."

even save money because doing so overworks the motor and shortens its life in the long run.

Remember Rule 8: Dirt is the enemy of moving parts. A vacuum motor has moving parts and it's certainly involved with dirt, so keep filters that protect the motor meticulously clean. These filters are quite inexpensive. Considering that they are so important to the life of the vacuum motor, replace them whenever they start to look the least bit dirty.

Most vacuums depend on rubber belts to transfer motion from the motor to the beater head. This belt wears out for various reasons, but the most common is just plain old age. "Old" for a vacuum belt may be less than a year. Belts take a real beating when you vacuum up something that stops the beater head from spinning (e.g., rug tassels, a paper clip, a piece of

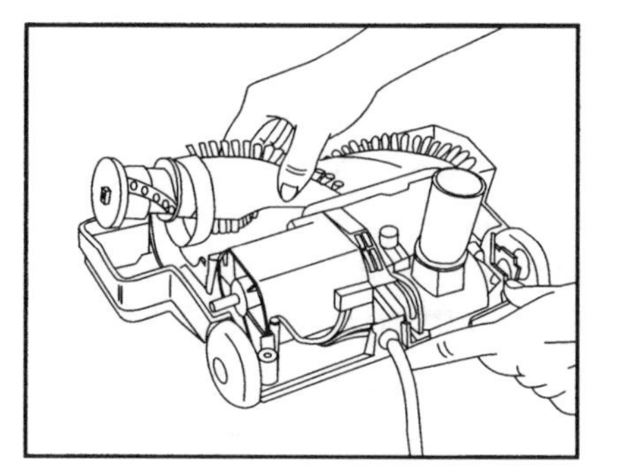

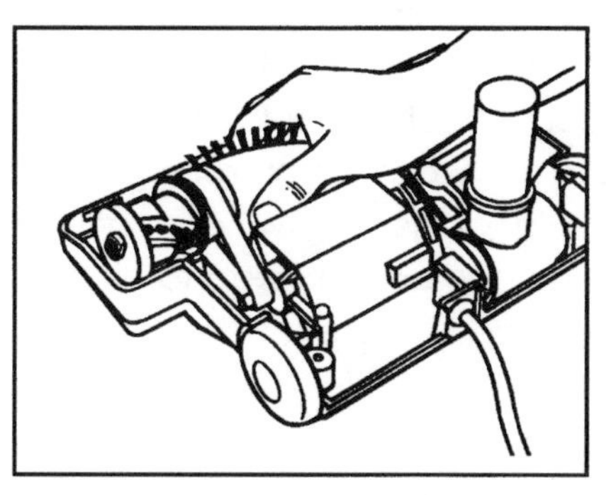

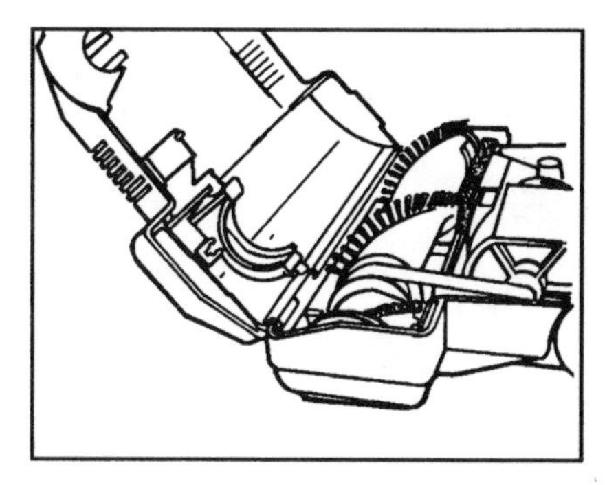

string, too many Christmas tree needles). Since the motor continues to run, the belt can heat up, become glazed, and/or melt. Some belts don't break; they merely loosen and quit working. Even if you somehow *don't notice* (!) that the vacuum is no longer picking anything up, you should be able to hear that the motor sounds different when the belt is broken or loose and the beater head is no longer turning at all or is turning at a much slower speed. Listen for the difference. Also learn to change a belt. The first step is to keep one on hand. See the illustrations on pages 178–179 or your owner's manual for typical belt-changing steps. While you're poking around in the vacuum changing the beater belt, clean misguided dirt, lint, string, gravel, hair, and so on, from anyplace you find it.

After each use or at least regularly, flip the beater head over and remove hair or string wrapped around the beater bar itself and where the bar attaches at each end. Insert a knife under the hair and string, and twist to loosen or cut it. Inspect the brushes on the beater bar and replace them when they are worn. If you replace them, replace them all—not just some.

To avoid clogs: (1) When vacuuming heavy accumulations, slow down. Allow the beater head to pick up everything in its path and regain its normal speed before moving on. (2) Don't even try to save time by vacuuming up paper clips, pins, collections of leaves or pine needles, anything wet, carpet fringes, rocks, marbles, wire, and the like. An otherwise innocent toothpick, for example, will create a clog when it lodges halfway

through the hose and other items start collecting around it. As already mentioned, notice what the vacuum normally sounds like because its pitch gets higher when it's clogged. If you continue to vacuum in spite of a clog, you will burn out the motor or ruin a belt in short order. It's the equivalent of a car attempting to pull too heavy a trailer up a mountain. The car's engine will work as hard as it can, but will make no progress and eventually will burn up.

To unclog the beater head of a canister vacuum or an upright vacuum, you must dismantle it—usually the same way you would when changing a beater bar belt. If the clog is in the neck of the vacuum leading to the dust bag, you may have to dismantle it further and/or remove the dust bag. If the clog is in the flexible hose of a canister, try to remove the clog by first disconnecting the hose from the vacuum. Then turn the hose around and hold its reverse end to the air intake of the vacuum and let the vacuum suck the clog back out. If that doesn't work, try using a broom handle or something similar to push the clog back out—in other words, insert the broom handle from the direction opposite the airflow. If the broom handle is too short, try a garden hose instead (without water, of course).

When you unplug the vacuum, don't try to save time by pulling the plug out of the wall from the vacuum end of the cord. This doesn't actually save any time because the plug will eventually break or the cord will short-circuit. Speaking of the plug, if your vacuum has an automatic rewind, don't let the cord come speeding back into the machine. The mechanism will eventually break when the plug end of the cord stops the rewind mechanism abruptly. Hold the cord and guide it into the rewind mechanism in a controlled manner.

Don't (unless you have a wet/dry vacuum) attempt to vacuum up water or anything remotely moist.

VCRs (Video Cassette Recorders)

Manufacturers used to advise us to clean VCR heads once a year as preventive maintenance. Since then, changes in tape formulations and equipment have led to a different rule of thumb: *Don't* clean them unless you have to. The heads are usually clogged by damp, worn-out, or cheap videotapes (which is often a roundabout way of saying rental tapes). If you don't play such tapes, your VCR may run for years without having to clean the heads. So proper maintenance is pretty simple: Use tapes with a reputable brand in good condition, and keep them that way by proper storage (see **Videotapes,** page 185). Otherwise, protect the unit from spills, allow air to circulate around it, and vacuum vents when you do your normal vacuuming. Shoo the cat or dog away from the unit so fur doesn't accumulate within. If you play a steady stream of rental tapes, you may have to count on more frequent maintenance.

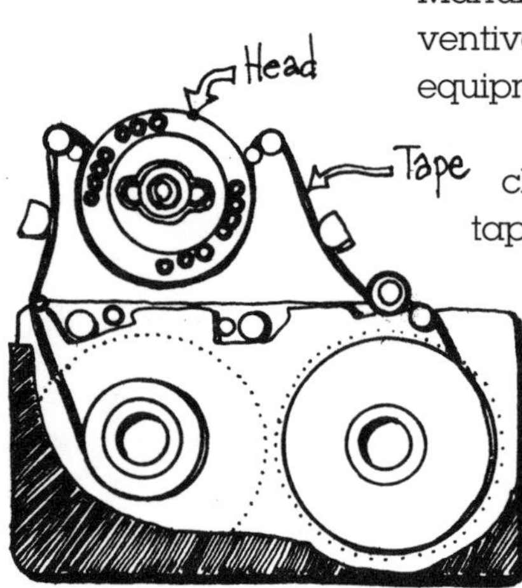

Dry and wet head-cleaning cassettes are available, but these days experienced VCR technicians don't recommend either one. In fact, quite often a VCR doesn't have a problem until the owner pops in a cleaning cassette. When we asked Keith Bianchi, who has been in the audio/video business since 1953, for his advice, he replied without hesitation, "*Leave it alone!*" In his experience, heads are most likely to clog when they run over a crease in a rental tape left there by the previous renter, who tried to smooth it over and didn't fess up to it when he or she returned the tape. These create a "death trap waiting for the next VCR," says Bianchi. He finds that when the instructions for a wet-cleaning tape say "add two drops of cleaning fluid," most of us figure "Well, if two drops are good, twenty are better." And then the excess fluid oozes all over the place and ruins the bearings on the tape guides.

So if you shouldn't use cleaning cassettes, how *do* you clean VCR heads? Daniel Bennett, owner of Omega Television in San Francisco, who has been repairing VCRs since they were first introduced, believes hand and professional cleaning are both safer than a head-cleaning cassette. But both Bennett and Bianchi agree that the best single thing you can do in case of a head clog is to play a new, high-quality tape for a while. The mild abrasion involved in playing a tape usually scrapes off—by the gentlest means possible—the oxides that have accumulated on the VCR heads. Buy a EXG-, HGK-, or PRO-grade 120-minute tape, fast-forward and rewind it to repack the tape, and then play it for anywhere from 15 to 120 minutes. If this doesn't clear the heads, head for the shop.

Video Camcorders

To keep them working in good condition for as long as possible, avoid using them in very dusty, humid, or wet conditions. When you move from hot to cold or cold to hot areas, allow time for the unit's temperature to adjust before operating. Don't aim at the sun or very bright light, both of which can ruin a camcorder's sensitivity to low light. According to Sony Hawaii, this can happen even when you're not using your camcorder—when it's strapped over your shoulder and the viewfinder is by chance pointed directly toward the sun. The viewfinder acts like a magnifying glass and focuses the sun's light, burning a large permanent spot. This is an expensive repair. Don't leave a camcorder in a hot car for any length of time. If you have to protect it during use and its case isn't handy, pop it into a plastic bag.

Remove the battery pack after use (see **Batteries**). Most camcorders have two batteries: a main battery and a clock battery. According to Keith Bianchi, who has been in the electronics business since long before camcorders were invented, if the main battery is left in place, the camcorder will switch to the main battery to run the clock—at least until it's drained to 1.3 volts. Then it switches back to the smaller clock battery, but by then it will have drained the main battery. And when you reach for the camcorder . . . well, you know the rest.

To clean the lens, first remove grit and dust with compressed air or a soft lens brush, or blow on it. Then apply lens-cleaning fluid or breathe on it, and wipe with a lens tissue or a clean soft cloth.

Most maintenance tasks that apply to full-size VCR units also apply to camcorders (see **VCRs,** page 182). But, as Mr. Bianchi observed, you would do well to remember that camcorders must be treated far more gently than full-size VCRs. For one thing, their motors and other critical parts are much smaller. If you encounter a sudden problem in a previously well-functioning camcorder, there are two things to try before heading for the repair shop: (1) Try a different or a new tape. If a tape exceeds the camcorder's tolerances even slightly, it can activate the camcorder's self-protective defenses, and the machine will shut down. (2) Turn off the automatic features (e.g., autofocus) and try to operate it again on manual settings. This may take care of the problem instantly. (Automatic functions on camcorders are not always reliable.)

Videotapes

No matter how expensive your VCR is, the quality of its picture and sound will be only as good as the tape you use. You can easily spend much more getting your VCR fixed or cleaned than you save by using bargain tapes. In order of increasing quality, the classes of tape include HG (High Grade), SHG (Super High Grade), EXG or HGK (Extra High Grade), and PRO (Professional). The higher the grade, the fewer the dropouts and (sometimes) the better the oxide coating and/or binder. Consumer magazines review VHS tapes from time to time, but within the video industry the buzz is that it's hard to go wrong with Fuji tapes.

According to Sony Hawaii, the signs of worn or creased tapes include:

1. thin black or white lines that practically fill up the screen during play mode with "snow";
2. a persistent noise heard at the same time the picture is distorted. When the noise goes away, so does the picture distortion.

Stop the tape where there's a problem. Flip open the cassette protection lid or gate and examine the tape at an angle. You should see a smooth dark surface, free of creases or dark streaks.

Keep a spare tape on hand so you can immediately replace a tape whenever it shows signs of decay. Better yet, use seven tapes—one for each day of the week—which will head off family crises that arise when someone (not you, of course) tapes over a program that someone else hadn't watched yet. Replace all seven when one of them starts to wear out, or after about two hundred record/play sessions.

Dirty rental tapes can quickly gum up the VCR's heads. If a rental tape has creases, wrinkles, or segments where the picture has been scraped off by too long a pause, stop the tape and don't rewind it. Return it as is and ask for a credit. If any tape can't be ejected from the VCR after a number of nonforceful attempts, it's by far safer to leave it in the VCR and take both in to be serviced.

Leaving a tape on pause for longer than thirty seconds or so can damage the tape as well as clog a VCR's heads. As Mr. Bianchi observed, tape heads are small but also sharp as knives, and they rotate at around 1,800 rpm. Most newer machines will take themselves off pause after a while, but why tempt fate?

Uneven tension can harm a tape, so it's generally not a good idea to store a tape stopped in the middle of its run. It's also best to eject a tape before shutting off the machine (i.e., don't leave it in the machine overnight). Before they record on a new tape, dedicated videophiles fast-forward and rewind a tape fully to release any tension in the tape created by adverse storage conditions (e.g., cooking and/or freezing in a freight car for a few weeks).

Store tapes on any edge (just not lying flat on its side) to minimize settling, misalignment, and damage to the edges of the tape. Invest in dust- and moisture-resistant cases for your prized tapes. These are now available at all sorts of stores and video rental outlets. Don't store tapes where significant moisture is present (e.g., in a damp basement or near an open window). Mildew may form, and moisture softens the tape surface so the heads can more easily scrape off a layer or two of oxide. Don't play a tape that you even suspect is damp or significantly cooler than room temperature.

To avoid a variety of problems, it's wise to "exercise" an unplayed tape at least once a year. Fast-forward it to the end, stop the tape, and eject it. Next year you can rewind it.

Wallpaper

The most important maintenance step is to control moisture, which can rapidly shorten the useful life of wallpaper. Open windows, use the exhaust fan, or install a dehumidifier to remove and control moisture. Please see the information on furniture placement and for water stains in **Walls and Ceilings,** immediately below.

Walls and Ceilings

Touch up painted walls regularly. Keep some leftover paint from each paint job specifically for this purpose. You can make the paint last much longer if you transfer the leftover paint into a quart container. Even better, transfer it into several pint-size cans. Empty cans are available from paint stores. Label and date each can. Use inexpensive throw-away paint brushes that are nothing more than a bit of foam rubber on a stick. You can get several of them for a dollar. Whenever there is a ding or scratch or mark, dab it away. You will keep an old paint job looking like new for years if you do.

Protect walls from furniture banging into them. Situate the furniture far enough away to prevent banging, or put a piece of wood between the wall and the furniture legs to prevent movement. Or add a rail to the wall at chair height. With wooden or plastic corner beads, you can protect wall corners from being dinged again and again. They are available at home-supply or hardware stores.

Look for water stains, especially below an exterior window or on the ceiling below a bathroom. They may indicate a need for weather-stripping or caulking around the window, or for plumbing repairs in the bathroom.

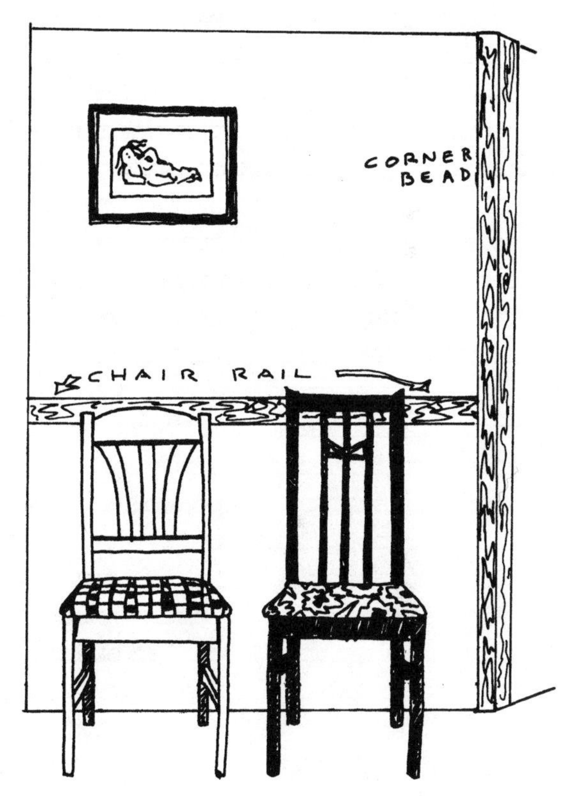

Washing Machines

Ever notice how the tops of many washers are corroded and rusted? Such damage is usually caused by laundry products. Soaps and detergents are corrosive when spilled and left moist for periods of time. Chlorine bleach, ammonia, stain removers, rust removers, and prewash sprays can be even worse. Wipe up such exterior spills, drips, and dribbles promptly. If any of these products find their way to rubber parts (e.g., the door gasket), rinse them off with water or Red or Blue Juice and then wipe. Don't use the washer top as a workplace for stain removal. Perform such operations over a sink and rinse it afterward.

Most owner's manuals tell us to turn off the hot and cold water faucets between uses to reduce pressure on the filler hoses and thereby reduce the possibility of the hoses bursting. These are sensible and prudent reasons, but I've yet to meet anyone who does this. My experience has been that I would have to move the washer even to be able to reach these faucets. Besides, plumbing expert Jeff Meehan says regularly turning the faucets on and off can, over time, actually loosen the valve spindle, which could then pop off and flood half of creation. This is eerily similar to the problem the owner's manuals want us to avoid!

Follow the owner's manual if you wish. Also inspect the hoses regularly for cracks, bulges, and splits. But my preference is to replace the plain rubber hoses with a new set of hoses wrapped in stainless steel mesh (approximately $22 a pair). Retighten new hoses at both ends after the first and second wash loads. Replace even stainless steel hoses every five to seven years. As added insurance, do turn off the hot and cold water faucets when you go on vacation. A broken hose while you're away can cause spectacular damage. (Close your eyes and visualize what your hardwood floors would look like under two inches of hot water.)

For the ultimate in protection, have a plumber install a deep drip pan (with an overflow line to a drain) under the washer. Similar to what's installed under most water heaters to catch any leaking water, a drip pan is especially appropriate when the washer is installed on an upper floor.

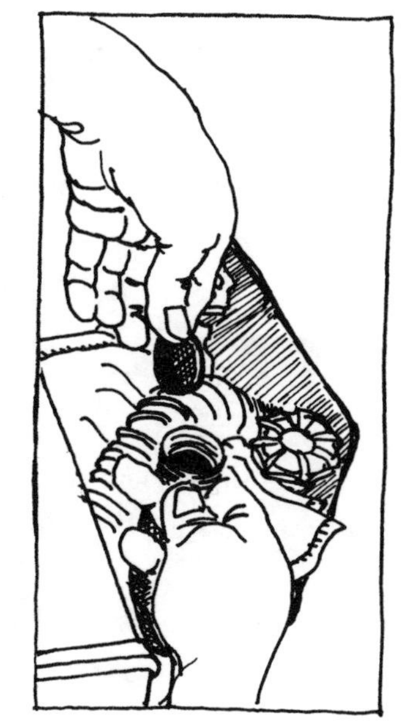

There is a filter washer on one or both ends of the hot and cold supply hoses. Even small amounts of debris caught in the screen will make the washing machine take forever to fill. Turn the water off, unscrew the hose, and use a screwdriver or needle-nose pliers gently to extract the filter washers. Keep a towel handy to catch the inevitable dribbles of water from the hoses. Clean with a toothbrush and by blasting water through the screen backward. Or just replace them (they're cheap) if they're difficult to clean or if they were punctured when you removed them. Be sure to check both ends of the hoses for filter washers. Check the filter washers if the washer takes longer than normal to fill with water, or whenever you replace the hoses.

Motor-driven appliances such as the washer should be level to help protect the motor bearings. In addition, for a washer at least, when the machine is in its spin cycle, it's important for it to be level to help keep it from vibrating or "walking." Walking is a major cause of failure of the filler hoses because the vibration or movement can stretch and stress them. Leave enough slack in the lines to allow for this (even if the washer is level).

Use a level to be sure your washer is installed properly. If you move the washer for any reason, relevel the machine when you put it back into position. At least the front two corners will each have a leveling foot. Place a level on the top of the washer. If only one leg isn't touching the floor, try extending that leg first by loosening the lock nut and then unscrewing the foot until it is solidly in contact with the floor. Often that's all you need to do. If not, adjust each leveling foot until the level bubble is centered front-to-back and side-to-side.

Don't change the controls of the washer (or dryer) while it is in midcycle. In other words, if you remember that you wanted to set it on the gentle cycle, but the machine is merrily proceeding though the normal cycle, don't just grab the dial and twist it to the new setting. First pull out the dial or whatever you do to stop the machine, and only then change to the new setting. The gears will appreciate it.

Don't habitually overload the machine. You may think you're getting away with it, but you're actually wearing out the machine at a much more rapid clip—including the gears in the transmission, which is the most expensive part of the machine. If the wash should be done in three loads, don't try to do it in two. Usually the owner's manual will list the machine's load capacity in pounds. But who has the time or scales to figure out the weight of a load? Instead, judge by the space the load takes up. Don't crowd. Mix small and large items together, and don't wrap large items around the agitator. Most of our mothers taught us to separate the wash by color. It also helps to separate lint producers (towels, chenille, throw rugs, etc.) from lint attractors (synthetics and permanent-press items). If your machine has a lint filter, clean it after each use.

Even though you've asked other family members to clean out their pockets before putting clothes in the hamper, check pockets before putting clothes into the washing machine. Washing coins can nick the enamel, and rust will get a foothold. Besides, one coin will eventually get stuck somewhere and have to be removed by a pro. Washing (and then especially drying) crayons or other items that melt or stain should also help convince us to take the time to check the contents of pockets before adding the item to the washer. Also zip up zippers and fasten hooks. **Note:** Appliance touch-up paint is available at appliance dealers and repair stores. If rust has already started, remove it with steel wool or sandpaper and prime the spot before repainting.

When you're done with the day's washing, leave the lid open at least long enough for the inside to dry completely. This helps prevent rust from getting started.

Water Heaters

A properly maintained water heater should last thirteen to twenty years. Considering that a replacement can cost upwards of $1,500, it's important to extend its life as long as possible.

A service agreement with a local company to perform annual maintenance on the hot water heater, the furnace, and the air conditioner is an excellent value. It may even be worth it to have three separate service agreements, but if you can find a company that can do all three or more, it's well worth the peace of mind.

Maintenance books and owner's manuals recommend that hot water heaters be drained (flushed)—either partially or fully—every six months to a year. Few homeowners bother to do this. Even if the homeowner is willing, the heater may or may not be easy to drain even though all water heaters have a hose connection and drain valve at the bottom. And, as expert San Francisco plumber Jeff Mehan has found time after time, the drain valve can become clogged with accumulated debris as the water heater is drained, which makes it difficult or impossible to reclose. Also, unfortunately, the drain valves used on most water heaters are notoriously poor in quality. The result is an emergency phone call to a plumber.

Especially if the water heater hasn't been drained in several years, draining it may cause more problems than it solves. Unless you started a regular draining schedule within the first year or so of a water heater's installation, I recommend having a plumber do it for you, at least for the first time. Also have the plumber check the drain valve and replace it with a higher-quality one if needed (a full-port gate valve), as well as test the temperature/pressure relief valve (see page 196).

If you're ready to drain the water heater, here is how to do it:

1. Shut off the cold-water supply to the tank.
2. If it's an electric heater, turn off the power. If it's a gas heater, turn the water temperature dial to the pilot or vacation setting.
3. Screw a garden hose onto the drain valve, and position the other end at a suitable drain site. (If a garden hose is not feasible, drain the tank into a bucket only until the water runs clear—not until the heater is completely empty, as in the following directions.)
4. Open the drain valve. When the tank is empty, turn the cold-water supply on and off a few times to create a few blasts into the tank to wash out additional sediment from the bottom of the tank.

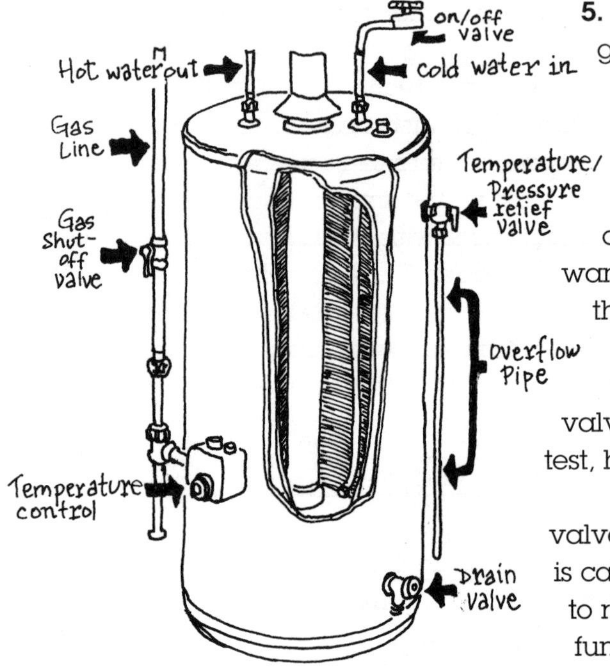

5. Close the drain valve, refill the tank, and reset the gas or turn the power back on.

The usual recommendation is to operate the temperature/pressure relief valve once every six months or year. As with draining, however, a bit of sediment can lodge in the valve and prevent its closing. If you want to perform this test, lift the pressure valve stem (near the top of the tank) for a second or two, and allow some water or air to escape. A good time to do this is when you've just refilled the tank with cold water. If the valve doesn't release properly or if it won't reseat after the test, have the heater serviced immediately.

Whether you drain the water heater and test the relief valve or not, a service visit from a plumber every few years is called for. They can do a more thorough kind of service to rid the heater of mineral buildup and also check other functions of the water heater. If the unit is taking an unusually long time to heat, if the water just won't get hot enough, and especially if you hear a crackling/rumbling sound as it heats the water, it's definitely time to call a plumber.

Here's other maintenance you should perform:

1. Vacuum around the base for dust, dirt, and lint on a regular basis.

2. Visually inspect the venting system of gas water heaters. Look for obstructions, damage, or deterioration of the venting cap or pipe, or rust flakes around the top of the water heater. Remove any obstructions: It's amazing the things someone might have left on top of it during the preceding year. If you see rust flakes or deterioration of the vent, call the utility company or a plumber to clean and replace the flue and venting system.

3. Inspect the burner in gas water heaters. Check for sooting, which is not normal and impairs proper combustion. If you find soot, call either the utility company or a plumber to service the unit.

4. Insulate it. If the water heater feels warm to the touch, it will work less and last thus longer if you install a water-heater blanket. Kits are available at most home-improvement and hardware stores. A blanket with an insulation value of at least R-11 is recommended. Newer water heaters are already insulated and don't need a blanket, so check the manufacturer's guidelines and warranty criteria before adding more insulation. (A blanket may actually void the warranty.) *Do not* insulate the top or bottom of gas water heaters. Insulation can interfere with the flue draft and/or cut off air to the pilot light. Insulate only the sides. However, the top and bottom of an electric water heater *should* be insulated.

Here are other energy-saving things you can do to lighten the load on the water heater and so help to lengthen its life:

1. Insulate the hot-water pipes. Your home is a good candidate for insulation if you use hot water frequently, if the pipe runs are long, and if the pipes pass through an uninsulated crawl space or basement.
2. Make sure the water temperature setting is correct: 120°F to 140°F meets most household needs. This is a setting between "low" and "medium" on most water heaters. (See **Dishwashers** for instructions on measuring the temperature of the hot water.)
3. Turn it to the lowest temperature setting (often labeled "vacation") when you leave for a week or more.

Water Softeners

A modern water softener doesn't require much maintenance other than keeping the unit properly filled and refilled with salt. Clean out the salt compartment before each refill. Wash the brine intake with a toothbrush and fresh water. Empty any brine or salt residue (or use a wet/dry vacuum) and rinse with fresh water. Turn off the water softener's timer and turn it to "bypass" mode when you go on vacation.

Water Supply

Once a year, test the main water supply shutoff valve by closing and opening it to be sure it hasn't stuck in the open position. Do the same thing with fixture shutoff valves that supply water to sinks and toilets. Both the main valve and fixture valves must be operable so water can be turned off in an emergency or when plumbing repairs are necessary. Label these valves so you and others can relocate them next year.

Pipes. If the hot-water pipes are covered with insulation, inspect them annually. Replace or reposition loose insulation, but be careful. If it's not visibly the do-it-yourself type of tubular insulation, and especially if it is old and looks like it contains plaster, there's a good chance it also contains asbestos. In such a case, consult a plumber or asbestos-abatement contractor. (Also see **Drains, Faucets, Sinks, Toilets,** and **Water Heaters.**)

Whirlpool Baths

Most are made of fiberglass, so don't use abrasive cleansers. Be patient when filling the tub, and wait until all the jets are covered by water before you start the motor. If the motor operates dry, you run the risk of burning it out. Use no soap—or minimal amounts of it—while the whirlpool is operating. Occasionally rinse interior pipes after use by refilling the tub with fresh water and turning on the motor. Once or twice a year, open and vacuum the compartment that contains the motor and the motor vents.

Windows

To continue to have easy-to-open, easy-to-slide windows, you should clean and lubricate them regularly. Open crank, awning, or jalousie windows to expose the extension arm. Remove dried grease, paints, and so on, with a wire brush. Clean with Red Juice and wipe dry. Spray a Teflon (or other) lubricant on the moving parts. (Use a piece of paper to keep the lubricant off painted areas.) Sliding window runners should be vacuumed with the crevice tool. Spray lubricant can be applied also. Wood windows will continue operating smoothly if you apply a very thin layer of paste wax or paraffin.

Caulking and/or weather-stripping windows and doors saves money and makes the house more comfortable. I've read that an eighth-inch opening around two door frames lets in as much cold air as a twelve-inch window opened six inches. The money you spend on caulking and weather-stripping is usually recovered in one heating season or less. And your home will be noticeably more comfy and cozy come winter. But most important, a house must remain waterproof to avoid the very serious problems water can cause when it gets into walls and floors.

Caulk around exterior window and door frames where they meet the siding. Weather-stripping should be applied around a window or doorjamb or at its threshold. Caulk is flexible when applied, but it eventually cracks, dries out, and has to be replaced. Weather-stripping materials include vinyl, rubber, metal, and foam rubber, most of which can also dry out or wear out and need periodic replacement.

Pick a day to caulk outdoors that is neither too hot nor too cold. Easier said than done, but it's downright impossible to caulk properly except in moderate and dry weather.

Caulking Instructions. Everything must be clean or the caulk won't adhere properly and you'll be wasting your time. Remove the old caulk (at least as much as is possible), loose paint, and dirt. Use a scraper, a wire brush, or sandpaper, depending on the surface. Apply caulk with a caulking gun or a pressurized can (see **Tub/Shower Enclosures,** page 22, for additional information). Get the best silicone caulk that money can buy. This is not the place to save a buck or two. Besides, it's a false savings. Cheap caulk will have to be replaced more quickly, which automatically multiplies its actual price—and that's nothing compared to the value of your time.

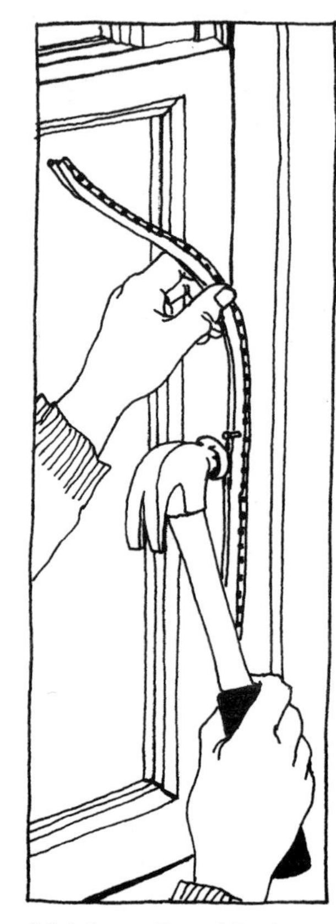
Metal weather stripping.

Fill any deep cracks with expanding foam sealant to within one-fourth to one-half inch of the surface, and use caulk as a top layer. Cut off about a half inch of the cartridge tip at a 45-degree angle, and puncture the interior seal with a nail. You can use the nail later as a stopper for any unused caulk. Don't caulk around the front door or the most prominent window first. Start where your work won't be noticed, because you won't be as skilled on the first door and window as you will be on later ones. However, with a steady hand and a little practice it's relatively simple to learn how to lay a uniformly wide bead that overlaps both sides for a good seal. Finish the job with a moistened finger, plastic spoon, or finishing tool (which you can buy at the same store where you bought the caulk and caulking gun). While you're in the mood, check for any openings or cracks around dryer vents, water pipes, exhaust fan outlets, lighting fixtures, window air conditioners, heating and cooling ductwork, garage doors, attic doors, and wires. Also check where porches attach to the house, the foundation, water spigots, TV cable, telephone lines, AC wires, seams between masonry and siding, chimney bricks and siding, and corners. Any opening should be sealed with caulk, foam sealant, gaskets, or weather-stripping. Try to seal things (pipes or wires, for example) that penetrate a wall both on the inside and the outside.

If you feel a draft of air between a window and its frame, the gap should be sealed with weather-stripping. (Air entering between the window frame and the wall indicates the need for caulk.) There are a number of choices, but the most durable (and most expensive) weather-stripping products are the smartest choices. They include bronze, aluminum, steel, rubber, and adhesive foam strips.

Condensation on the inside of windows or between windows and storm windows is another indication of the need to weather-strip (or to add storm windows). If you do caulk around storm windows (which may make them inoperable), make sure the weep holes at the bottom of the storm window frame are clear so moisture can escape. You can also reduce condensation by turning on the bathroom and kitchen exhaust fans. High humidity in the house contributes to buildup of condensation on cold surfaces like windows. It's worth checking the indoor relative humidity in your home if it seems too humid to you. Around 30 percent to 50 percent relative humidity is optimal during the heating season.

Locate the origin of excess moisture, if present. A wet crawl space or basement may have to be covered or waterproofed. Moisture is also a byproduct of combustion. If you can't find any other source, have your heating system and chimney checked.

Sliding window tracks should be vacuumed at least once a year. These tracks generally have weep holes to allow rainwater to escape. Check to be sure they're clear as you vacuum. Teflon spray, paste wax, or paraffin may make opening or closing windows easy again.

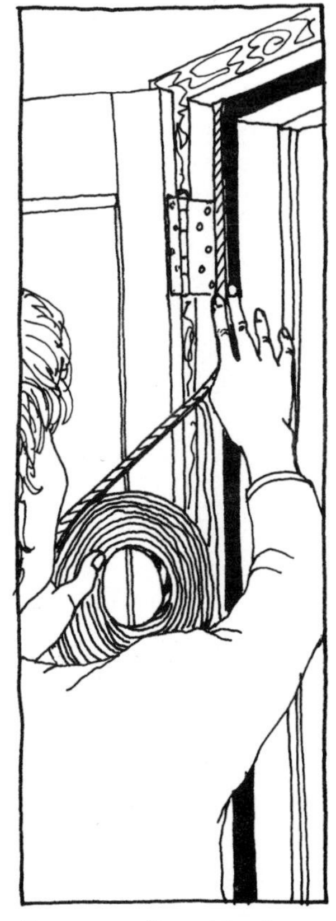

Foam weather stripping.

Wine

Maintenance of wine is not a concept that needs any particular discussion in my family—we drink it before the bottle even needs to be dusted. The same goes for any partial bottle left at the end of a meal. I suppose households with wine cellars don't spend time discussing wine maintenance either—at least once the cellar construction is complete. But there are a few maintenance considerations for the balance of the wine-drinking population.

Wine likes to be stored cool (the ideal is around 55°F), without frequent temperature fluctuations, and without vibration or frequent movement. Of course, this describes the wine cellar we all don't have, so just use this as a guide. The first choice for storage is a nice cool place. If you have a reasonably consistently cool place, store the wine there—in cardboard boxes to help insulate against temperature fluctuations. Storing on a concrete slab can help keep bottles cool. If you can't locate a consistently cool place, at least pick one that doesn't get hot. If you can't find a place like that, put your wine in the refrigerator (including red wines too), or at least keep them there during hot spells. Storage in a refrigerator is not a substitute for a wine cellar, and it should not be used for permanent wine storage. But the problems that arise from storing it there take a long time to develop, and they are less injurious to wine than letting it get cooked in a hot location.

Ideal storage involves laying the bottles on their side, with the cork end tilted slightly down.

There are a few options for maintaining partial bottles of red wines. Red wines start to taste like vinegar a day (more or less) after they're opened unless you take steps to preserve them. (For white wines, just replace the cork and store in the refrigerator.) Here are several choices for preserving a partial bottle of red wine:

1. Pour a half-full bottle into an empty *half* bottle and tightly recork. The less air left in the half bottle, the better. Oxygen in the air is what turns the wine into vinegar.
2. Wine authority Ronn Wiegand says to freeze it right in the bottle! When you're ready to finish it, let it thaw to room temperature. He says you can even microwave it to speed up the thawing as long as you don't let it get warm.
3. There are at least two inexpensive products that work. My personal favorite is Private Preserve

Wine Preserver. It's an aerosol can containing a safe, inert gas that blankets the wine as it forces out the offending air. Then just recork the bottle or use a special stopper to keep air out, and set it aside until you're ready to finish it. Heidi Yorkshire, author of *Wine Savvy* (Portland, Ore.: Duplex Media Group, 1995), favors a Vacu-Vin. It's a simple plastic device that allows you to pump most of the air out of the bottle. Special stoppers replace the cork and prevent air from getting back into the bottle. She says they'll keep for at least several days, which is similar to my experience with the Private Preserve Wine Preserver. Both products are available at wine specialty stores and by mail order from the Wine Enthusiast Catalog (1-800-356-8466).

Wrought Iron

Don't do anything with it other than keep it clean by dusting or wiping—unless it starts to rust. If that happens, remove the rust with steel wool or by chemical methods. Reprime and repaint. Depending on how long it took to start to rust in the first place, you may be able to retard the return of rust by applying a coat of liquid or paste wax. More important than a coat of wax is to be thorough when removing all the old rust before repainting.

Appendix A

CLEANING SUPPLIES

When maintenance calls for a cleaning product, we usually reach for the same safe, effective ones The Clean Team uses to clean San Francisco homes day in and day out. Since our favorite products might have names you're not familiar with, we promised in Chapter 1 to explain them further here. What follows is another alphabetical list, this time of some of the cleaning products and supplies mentioned in the preceding chapters.

Acrylic Floor Finish

Also referred to as "acrylic." Although it is often mistaken for a liquid wax, it is actually a type of liquid plastic floor finish. Examples are Future and the one we use, High-Gloss Acrylic Floor Finish.

Alcohol

It's not often used for regular housecleaning, but since it's used regularly in maintenance cleaning, especially on electronics equipment, here's a bit more information about it. Household alcohol (aka rubbing alcohol, isopropyl alcohol, and/or denatured alcohol), although okay for cleaning jobs that call for the use of alcohol, is not the *best* choice because it's only around 70 percent alcohol: 90 percent or 95 percent alcohol has fewer impurities, will leave less residue, and is better for cleaning. Purer alcohol formulations are also available at drugstores for just a little more money. These are all nondrinkable (denatured) varieties of alcohol, but according to audio expert Lewis Downs, vodka is also a very pure alcohol and can be used for cleaning jobs in a pinch. Finally, even though it may not be noticeable to you, alcohol ultimately dries out rubber, so try to avoid rubber parts when cleaning with alcohol, or at least use very small amounts of it on or around rubber. Better yet, purchase a specialized product such as TASCAM RC rubber cleaner.

Ammonia, Clear

An old-fashioned cleaner that is hard to improve upon. It's best without the addition of suds, which just slow you down without increasing ammonia's effectiveness. Suds also leave an unwanted residue. Use ammonia for washing windows, mirrors, walls, ceilings, and floors. Use it in stronger ratios for very dirty floors, and all the way to full strength to remove heavy grease buildup and to strip wax or acrylic off floors.

Apron, Cleaning

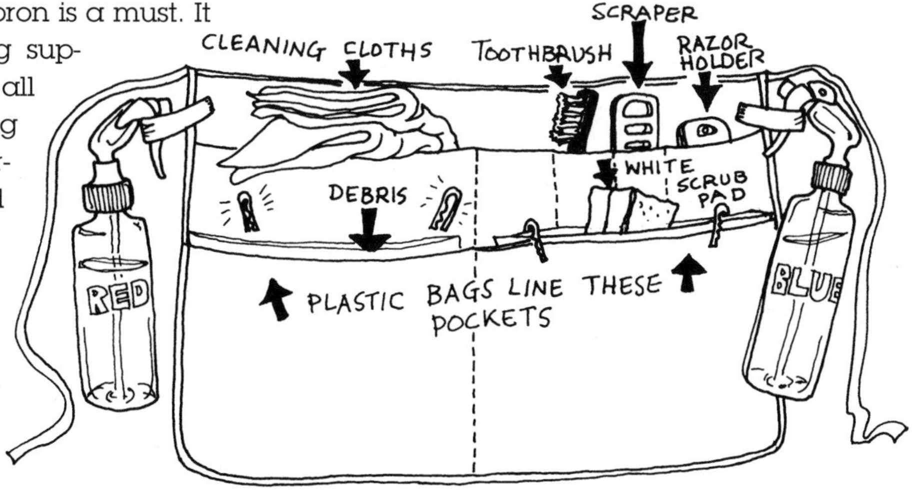

If you want to get the cleaning over with and move on to other things life has to offer, a cleaning apron is a must. It allows you to carry cleaning supplies with you and eliminate all that back-and-forth scurrying that wastes so much time. Carpenters don't run up and down a ladder every time they need another nail, do they? They wear a tool belt to save time. Why not wear something similar while cleaning? Its pockets and loops allow you to keep everything you need at

your fingertips as you work your way around a room—without having to backtrack. Avoiding this backtracking is the single most important step for efficient, speedy housecleaning. For some of the more specialized tasks described in this book, add the appropriate tool and/or cleaning agent for the duration of the task.

Blue Juice

The light-duty liquid cleaner used by The Clean Team. It is an industrial version of consumer products like Windex, Glass Plus, Formula 409 glass & surface, and other glass cleaners. Used mainly for cleaning glass: mirrors, picture glass, glass tables, etc.

Brushes

Brushes can increase the effectiveness of cleaning efforts many times over. They often last for years. Use them handheld or on a pole, depending on the job at hand. Here are some of the ones you'll find handy to have around:

Dusting: It's really a good paintbrush, with natural bristles and feathered ends, but don't call it that or it'll disappear. Use on wicker furniture, computer keyboards, lamp shades, picture frames, molding, stereo equipment, light fixtures, the tops of books, car dashboards, etc.

Stiff-bristled: Same idea as a *toothbrush*, but for bigger jobs. Used to scrub grout lines between glazed and paver tiles, concrete floors, and patio stones. Also for scrubbing floors, greasy bricks, stove hoods, and many other rough surfaces. One aging former member of The Clean Team with arthritic knees and a touchy back swears by this brush: Attached to a long handle with a 360-degree swivel head, it can scrub surfaces without the operator having to bend over or kneel down.

Soft-bristled: Use for wet-cleaning miniblinds, windows, and window screens.

Ceiling and wall: Use to remove spiderwebs and dust in high places.

Clean Team, The

Founded in 1979, The Clean Team Cleaning Service is San Francisco's busiest housecleaning service, cleaning around twenty thousand times a year. We developed a method of cleaning now known as Speed Cleaning. Founded in 1987, The Clean Catalog Company offers cleaning products that are tested and selected by professional housecleaners to consumers via our mail-order catalog. Many of the products mentioned here and in our previous books are available through this catalog.

Cleaning Cloth

Hundred-percent-cotton cleaning cloths are more absorbent, are strong enough to allow real scrubbing, and can be used over and over again. They save cleaning time, and they save money compared to the cost of all the rolls of paper towels that you would otherwise purchase during their lifetime. Use white clothes only: dye can transfer to surfaces being cleaned.

Green Scrub Pad (Green Pad) See **White Scrub Pad.**

Grout-Coloring Agent

Used to cover up permanent stains in grout lines. Not a cleaner, it's more like a coat of paint over dirty grout. It cannot replace missing grout, no matter how hard you try. Our product is called Grout Whitener.

Grout Sealer

A product used to fill the pores and microscopic cracks in grout so they won't collect dirt or stains instead. Sealer should be applied on all newly installed grout. Reapply it per the manufacturer's instructions, generally once or twice a year. Besides grout, many finely pitted surfaces benefit from a sealer. Stone, brick, cement, crazed (finely cracked) tile, and other nonglazed tiles are examples. Our product is called Grout Sealer.

HEPA

High-efficiency particulate air filter (often in three stages). A "true" HEPA filter will capture 99.97 percent of particles larger than 0.3 micron. But read the product's specs carefully: HEPA is a term applied somewhat overzealously these days. HEPA filters were originally developed to trap radioactive dust in atomic plants.

Rabbit-Ear Duster

An extension duster that can be bent to mimic the shape or angle of the surface to be dusted.

Red Juice

The heavy-duty liquid cleaner used by The Clean Team. It is an industrial version of consumer products like Fantastik, Mr. Clean, Pine-Sol, Simple Green, and Formula 409. As with our other favorites, Red Juice is by far the best one of this category we've ever found: It's nontoxic, odorless, biodegradable, and consistently excellent. Used to remove fingerprints, grease, and smudges of all kinds from countertops, walls, woodwork, shelves, cupboards, appliances, and many other surfaces. Also used to remove grease- and water-based stains from carpets and upholstery and to pretreat laundry.

Scraper

Carried in a cleaning apron to be at your fingertips for removing mystery globs on counters, floors, or other durable hard surfaces. Otherwise known as a putty knife. The new plastic ones are safer on more surfaces and so have greater utility, if not greater longevity.

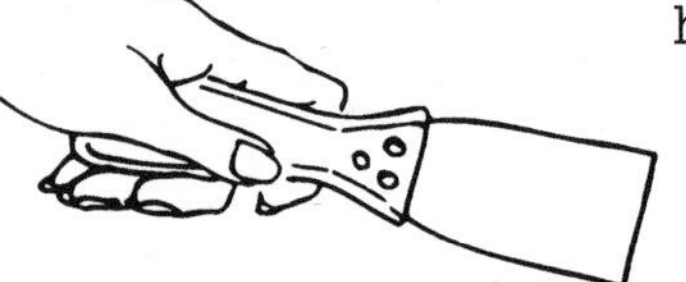

Tile Juice

The Clean Team's choice over things like Lime-A-Way, Dow bathroom cleaner, X-14, Shower Power, Lysol basin, tub, and tile cleaner, and so forth for removing hard water, soap scum, and heavy accumulation of plain old dirt from tubs and showers.

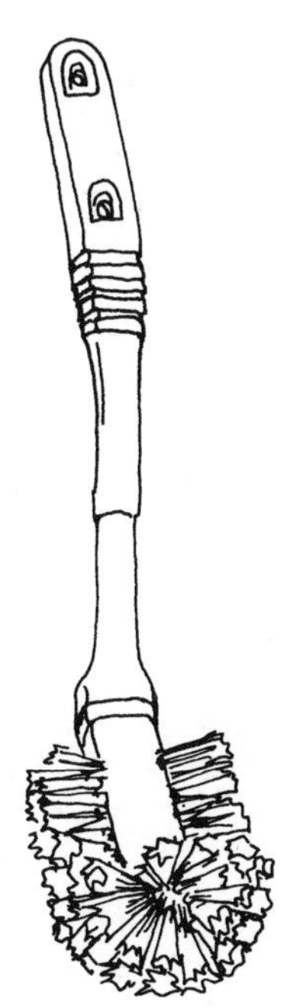

Toilet Brush

For even this simple household item, we have strong opinions about what works and what doesn't work. The best ones—which luckily enough are often the least expensive—are all plastic (no twisted wire), have stiff bristles for good scrubbing action, are shaped to reach deep into the toilet neck and under the toilet rim, and have a handle long enough to keep the user satisfyingly distant.

"Toothbrush"

It looks like a dental toothbrush, but it's really a serious cleaning tool that can clean practically anything *but* teeth. It has strong bristles and a shape that allows you to scrub without banging your knuckles in the process.

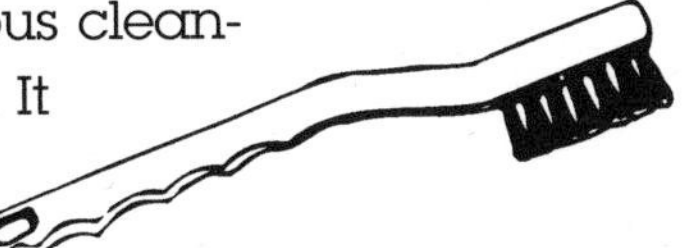

Vinegar, White

White vinegar is 5 percent acetic acid—the mildest acid available. Sometimes suggested as a floor cleaner or as a safer alternative cleaner for removing hard-water deposits in the shower. It's not particularly effective for either of these jobs because it's so mild. This mildness can be overcome when something with hard-water deposits can be soaked in it. Examples are showerheads or deposits in vases. It's acidic, so don't use it on marble. White vinegar can also be used in a dishwasher to remove stains.

White Scrub Pad (White Pad)

A modern abrasive material, usually a sponge on one side and a white pad on the other. Use when a cleaning cloth or toothbrush aren't strong enough. It's far less likely to scratch a surface than any other color pad (e.g., green, black, etc.), yet it's almost as effective for most household uses. Use wet, and make sure you're not pressing so hard that you're scratching the surface. Also offered by 3M (Scotch Brite), O-Cel-O, and S.O.S.

How to Order Tools, Equipment, and Supplies

The Clean Team Catalog offers the products The Clean Team Housecleaning Company actually uses. Because we use cleaning products daily and test new ones regularly, we know what works and won't tolerate anything that doesn't.

One way to save time in your own housecleaning is to skip all the tests and trials of products that we do. But even if you know what products you want to use, it still takes time to purchase them—especially if they're not carried at the local grocery or hardware store, as is true of many of the professional products we use. Our catalog can save you time on both accounts, because you can make your choices without leaving your home. The only products we offer are the best ones we've found so far—and we're still looking after nearly twenty years.

If you would like a free copy of our catalog, please write us at:

The Clean Team
206B N. Main St.
Jackson, CA 95642

If you prefer, please call us at 1-800-238-2996 and we'll mail you one the same day. Or call us anytime for solutions to your toughest cleaning problems.

Or visit our Web site at:

www.thecleanteam.com

Appendix B

REFERENCES

If you're feeling a need for more detailed information, here are a few sources for you to explore—via the Internet as well as plain old magazines and books. Our apologies in advance if the Web sites are inoperative: It is the nature of Web sites to be in transition. And we are being by no means thorough here: reference sources are scattered far and wide, but these are among our favorites.

Web Sites

www.msue.msu.edu/msue/iac/iacmain.html This terrific site is operated by Michigan State University Extension. It is the A–Z Great-grandmother of All Web Sites for home care and maintenance. After reaching the home page, click on FAMILY RESOURCE MANAGEMENT (twice), then HOME MAINTENANCE AND REPAIR DATABASE, then HOME MAINTENANCE AND REPAIR.

www.popularmechanics.com An exceptionally well-organized site, this is the Web site of *Popular Mechanics* magazine. From the home page, click HOME IMPROVEMENT, then HOMEOWNER'S CLINIC or SMART CONSUMER or HOME IMPROVEMENT (again).

www.onthehouse.com This is the Web site of the Associated Press syndicated column ("On the House") by James and Morris Carey. Always a pleasure to read, the Carey brothers' columns are clear, thorough without being overwhelming, and well illustrated. They usually discuss repair and remodeling projects, but their maintenance articles are right on target. From the home page, click on NEWSPAPER COLUMN or TIP OF THE WEEK. Or enter "maintenance" as a search term.

www.pacificharbor.com/whpier/pdd The Web site of Pete Prlain, who hosts a syndicated TV and radio show called "How-to with Pete." It offers direct, helpful, and down-to-earth entries on maintenance. From the home page, click on HOW TO or ASK PETE at the bottom of the page.

www.hometime.com This is the Web site of the TV series *Hometime*. From the home page, click on HOME MAINTENANCE or go to the bottom of the home page, click on SITE SEARCH, and enter "maintenance" as a search term.

For AOL subscribers Click on KEYWORD on the top bar, then type "HouseNet." Click on the HOME IMPROVEMENT image (not title). All sorts of topics will pop up. REPAIR/MAINTENANCE is particularly helpful.

mkennedy@primenet.com For help with scratched compact discs, contact the Compact Disc Repairman at this e-mail address.

www.service@sonyhawaii.com A good source for answers to your questions about electronic equipment.

www.ge.com/appliance This is the Web address for the GE Parts Master Program. Contact them with the name and number of the appliance for which you need parts.

Magazines

Fans of hers will already know this, but *Martha Stewart Living* can be a gold mine of information on home maintenance. Articles on the subject can be found anywhere in the magazine, but they are typically found in the "Homekeeping" section. Ms. Stewart and her staff are particularly good at finding and interviewing just the right expert (often with decades of experience).

Another essential magazine for home maintenance is *This Old House*. Not an issue goes by without a tantalizing article on a major maintenance topic. They are especially well researched and illustrated. As with *Martha Stewart Living*, a resource section will guide you to sources of products mentioned in the articles. And the more traditional sources should not be overlooked either—especially *Popular Mechanics*. Their regular "Homeowner's Clinic" department is usually the place to check.

Our Previous Books

We couldn't resist the temptation to give our own books a great big mention. Besides, they're chock full of good information for any busy person having to deal with any aspect of housekeeping in the busy 90's and beyond.

Speed Cleaning (New York: Dell Publishing, 1985): The cleaning trade secrets of The Clean Team became our first book. It has become a bible to many, and is still a perennially steady seller. *Speed Cleaning* shows you how to finish weekly or every-other-week cleaning in minutes instead of hours. It has put leisure back into weekends for families all over the country. Also in Italy, England, Canada, and Australia.

Spring Cleaning (New York: Dell Publishing, 1989): This book teaches you how to do the bigger, but thankfully less frequent, jobs with skill and efficiency.

Clutter Control (New York: Dell Publishing, 1992): Our third book addresses the subject of household organization: How to keep the house from being overwhelmed by paper, products, and other modern detritus, how to keep track of the things within the house, and how to keep the household civilized enough to tackle the weekly cleaning chores.

Talking Dirt (New York: Dell Publishing, 1997): The subtitle of this book is *America's Speed Cleaning Expert Answers the 157 Most-Asked Cleaning Questions.* People have been asking us questions about cleaning problems since our first book was published. We thought it was time to answer the most important ones for everyone.

Other Helpful Books

Herberle, Dave. *The Complete Guide to Four Season Home Maintenance.* Cincinnati: Betterway Publications, 1993.

Papolos, Janice. *The Virgin Homeowner.* New York: W. W. Norton & Co., 1997.

Peterson, Franklynn. *How to Fix Damn Near Everything.* New York: Bonanza Books, 1989.

Reader's Digest Book of Home Do It Yourself Projects. New York: Putnam, 1996.

Shep, Robert L. *Cleaning and Caring for Books.* London: Sheppard Press, 1982.

Yorkshire, Heidi. *Wine Savvy.* Portland: Duplex Media Group, 1995.

Index

Acrylic floor finish, 207
Aerators, 84–85
Air, indoor, 19–20
Air cleaners, 20–21
Air conditioners, 7
  central, 111–114
  window, 114–118
Air filters, electronic, 110–111
Alcohol, 208
Alkaline batteries, 25
Ammonia, clear, 208–209
Apron, cleaning, 209–210
Artificial plants, 137–138
Attic storage, 163
Audiotapes (*see* Cassette tapes)

Baseboard electric heaters, 107
Basement storage, 163
Bathtubs, 21–22
Batteries, 25–26
  cameras, 156
  smoke detectors, 156
  thermostat, 171
  video camcorders, 184–185
Bedding
  blankets, 27–28
  down comforters, 29
  electric blankets, 28–29
  pillows, 29–31
Belts, vacuum, 179–181
Blankets, 27–28
  electric, 28–29
Blenders, 31
Blinds, 126–128
Blue Juice, 49, 57, 60, 129, 131, 169, 172, 210
Books, reference, 221–222
Books and bookshelves, 31–33
Box fans, 76
Brushes, 210–211, 215
Butcher block surfaces, 33–35

Cabinets, 35–36
Camcorders (*see* Video camcorders)
Cameras, 36–37
Canned air, 37, 56, 57, 155, 171
Can openers, 38–39
Carpets, 15, 39–43
Cassette tape decks, 43–45
Cassette tapes, 45–46
Cast-iron cooking utensils, 46

Castors, 42
Caulking
  tub/shower enclosures, 22–25
  windows and doors, 200–203
CD players (*see* Compact disc players)
Ceiling fans, 76–79
Ceilings, 188–189
Cement floors, 88–89
Central air conditioners, 111–114
Ceramic tile, 46–47
Christmas trees, 47
Circuits, overloaded, 74
Cleaning apron, 209–210
Cleaning cloths, 49, 212
Cleaning supplies, 48–50, 207–217
Clean Team Cleaning Service, The, 11–12, 49, 211–212, 216–217
Closets, 50
Clothes dryers, 70–73
Clothes washers, 14, 80–84, 177, 190–194
Cloths, cleaning, 49, 212
Clutter Control, 11, 50, 221
Coffeemakers, 50–51
Coffee/spice grinders, 52
Comforters, down, 29
Compact disc players, 15, 52–53
Compact discs, 53–55
Compactors, trash, 176
Computer mouse, 57–58
Computers, 55–57
Convection ovens, 58
Cooking utensils, cast-iron, 46
Cordless telephones, 167
Countertops, 59
Creosote buildup, 87
Crystal display pieces, 59–60
Curtains, 60–61

Defrosting freezers, 90–91
Dehumidifiers, 20, 61, 136, 137
Dishwashers, 61–65
Distilled water, 121
Doors, sliding, 66–67
Doors and door hardware, 65–67
Down comforters, 29
Drain cleaners, 69–70, 101, 177
Drains, 21, 67–70, 101, 153, 154
Drapes, 60–61
Dried plants, 137–138
Dryers
  clothes, 70–73
  hair, 106
Dry rot, 170
Dust, 73
Dust mites, 123, 124

Electric blankets, 28–29
Electric heaters, 107–108
Electronic air filters, 110–111
Electronics, 75–76 (*see also* individual components)
Enamel stove tops, 164–165
Endust, 169
Exhaust or vent fans, 19, 79

Fabric furniture, 94
Fans
  box, 76
  ceiling, 76–79
  exhaust or vent, 19, 79
  oscillating, 76
Faucets, 79
  aerators, 84–85
  washers, 80–84
Fax machines, 85
Feather pillows, 29–30
Filters, 16, 19–21, 73

Filters (*cont.*)
central air conditioners, 113
electronic air filters, 110–111
furnace, 108
window air conditioners, 118
Fire extinguishers, 9–10, 85–86
Fireplaces, 87
Floor mats, 16–17, 39, 73, 161
Floors, 88–90
Food processors, 90
Freezers, 13–14, 90–92
Furnaces, 108–111
Furniture, 93–94
fabric, 94
glass, 99–100
leather, 94–97
wicker, 98–99
wood, 100–101

Garbage disposers, 101–105
Glass furniture, 99–100
Granite, 162
Graphite powder, 65–66
Greasy stains, 98
Green scrub pad (*see* White scrub pad)
Ground–fault circuit interrupters (GFIs or GFCIs), 73–74
Grout, 17, 47, 105–106
Grout-coloring agent, 212
Grout sealer, 213
Guardsman, 94

Hair dryers, 106
Hardware, door, 65–67
Heaters, electric, 107–108
Heaters, water, 64, 177, 191, 194–198
Heating system, 108–111
Heat pumps, 118
HEPA (high-efficiency particulate air) filters, 21, 213
High-maintenance items, 4–6
Hinges (*see* Doors and door hardware)
Hoods, stove, 166
Hot plates, 119
Humidifiers, 111, 119–120, 136, 137

Indoor plants, 138–141
Information sources, 218–222
Irons, 120–122

Journal, maintenance, 18

Kettles, 167

Lacquer finishes, 137
Lampshades, 122–123
Leaks, 15–16, 150 (*see also* Bathtubs, Faucets, Toilets)
Leather furniture, 94–97
Light fixtures, 123
Lightning arrester, 75
Limestone, 159, 162
Lint, from dryer, 70–73
Litter boxes, 135–136

Magazines, 220–221
Maintenance journal, 18
Maintenance rules, 13–18
Marble, 159, 162
Martha Stewart Living, 220
Mats, floor, 16–17, 39, 73, 161
Mattresses, 123–125
McRoskey Airflex Mattress Company, 124, 125

Microwave ovens, 126
Mildew, 20, 23, 24, 33, 65, 110, 144, 163
Mineral deposits, 50–51, 167
Miniblinds, 126–128
Mirrors, 128–129
Mixers, hand-held and standing, 129–130
Moisture, 20, 22, 33, 36–37, 169, 203
Mold, 20, 110, 119
Monitors, 57
Mouse, computer, 57–58
Moving parts, 16, 43, 179

Ni-Cad (rechargeable) batteries, 25–26

Oscillating fans, 76
Ovens, 130–131
  convection, 58
  microwave, 126
  toaster, 171–172
Overloaded circuits, 74

Paintings, 131–132
Pets, 132–136
Pewter, 136
Pianos, 136–137
Pillows, 29–31
Pipes, 199
Plants
  dry, natural, and artificial, 137–138
  indoor, 138–141
Plexiglas, 132
Plumber's snake, 68–69, 174
Plungers, 67–68, 174, 175
Polyurethane finishes, 32, 100–101
Popular Mechanics, 51, 221
Porcelain sinks, 154–155
Portable electric fan heaters, 107
Protectors
  cabinet doors, 36
  surface, 93–94
P-trap, 67, 83–84

Quarry tile, 89

Rabbit-ear dusters, 77, 213
Radiator oil heaters, 108
Red Juice, 12, 27, 31, 40, 41, 49, 58, 61, 101, 108, 129, 136, 137, 146, 162, 166, 167, 172, 175, 176, 200, 214
Refrigerators, 17, 141–147, 177
Remote controls, 148
Rice cookers, 158
Root-bound plants, 141
Rugs, 39–43

Scheduling maintenance, 13–14
Scotchguard, 43, 94
Scrapers, 214
Security systems, 148–149
Septic systems, 105, 149–151
Shampooing carpets, 40–42, 177
Showerheads, 151–152
Showers (*see* Bathtubs)
Shower/tub enclosures, 22–25
Silver, 152–153
Sinks, 153–154
  porcelain, 154–155
  stainless steel, 155
Slate, 162–163
Sliding doors, 66–67
Sliding window tracks, 203
Smoke detectors, 155–156
Smooth ceramic glass or black glass stove tops, 165–166
Soil retardants, 43
Speakers, 156–157

Speed Cleaning, 11, 48, 221
Spice/cofffee grinders, 52
Spring Cleaning, 11, 221
Stainless steel sinks, 155
Stains
  greasy, 98
  on natural stones, 162–163
  water-soluble, 98
Steamers, 158
Stone building materials, 158–163
Storage areas, 163
Stove hoods, 166
Stoves, 164
Stove tops
  enamel, 164–165
  smooth ceramic glass or black glass, 165–166
Sunlight damage, 16, 42, 60
Supplies, cleaning, 48–50
Surface protectors, 93–94
Surge protectors, 56, 168

Talking Dirt, 11, 123, 127, 162, 222
Teakettles, 167
Telephone answering devices, 168
Telephones, cordless, 167
Televisions, 168–169
Termites, 169–171
Terrazzo floors, 89
Thermostats, 171
This Old House, 220
Tile, ceramic, 46–47
Tile Juice, 49, 106, 215
Toasters and toaster ovens, 171–172
Toilet brush, 215
Toilets, 172–175
Toilet seats, 175–176
Toothbrushes, cleaning, 136, 215
Trash compactors, 176
Tub/shower enclosures, 22–25
TVs (*see* Televisions)

Uninterruptible power supply (UPS), 56

Vacation maintenance checklist, 177–178
Vacuum cleaners, 178–182
Vacuuming, 39, 88
VCRs (video cassette recorders), 182–184
Video camcorders, 184–185
Videotapes, 185–188
Vinegar, white, 216

Wallpaper, 188
Walls, 188–189
Walnut oil, 34–35
Warnings, 8–9
Washing machines, 14, 80–84, 177, 190–194
Water, 15–16, 22–24, 79–80
Water heaters, 64, 177, 191, 194–198
Watering plants, 139–140
Water softeners, 121, 159, 177, 198
Water-soluble stains, 98
Water supply, 199
Weather-stripping, 73, 200–203
Whirlpool baths, 199–200
White scrub pad, 216
White vinegar, 216
Wicker furniture, 98–99
Window air conditioners, 114–118
Window blinds, 126–128
Windows, 200–203
Wine, 204–206
Wood floors, 89–90
Wood furniture, 100–101
Wrought iron, 206